REFLECTIONS
ON DOOR COUNTY

A GRACE SAMUELSON
SAMPLER

VOYAGEUR PRESS

Published by Voyageur Press Incorporated
212 N. 2nd Street
Minneapolis, Minnesota 55401

ISBN-0-89658-062-8

Printed in the United States of America.

Table of Contents

Editor's Preface

Grace Samuelson has been writing and publishing for a long time, and there should have been a book of hers available long since. For a number of reasons, this is the first time that some of her work has been selected, arranged, and prepared for publication in one volume.

The prose pieces here included can speak for themselves. The first section "Reflections" is composed of miscellaneous pieces ranging from family history to description and anecdote. "Good Enough for the Help" contains eleven essays that describe the existence of the well-known and lamented "Samuelson's," a restaurant that lives on in the memories of many happy and well-fed Midwesterners, as well as the television work that occurred because of the restaurant and Grace Samuelson's way with food.

The third section, "A Year from the Past," needs some explanation. For a number of years the *Door County Advocate*, the twice-weekly newspaper published in Sturgeon Bay, Wisconsin, has printed a monthly feature in which Grace reminisces about that month in years and times gone by. The series has become one of the most popular on-going parts of the newspaper, and no selection from her work would be complete without a chronicle of the months. The twelve months included in this volume have been selected from a number of possibilities; thus, the year presented is "constructed" and is not a previously published sequence.

Fiction and poetry have been excluded from this selection for the purpose of unity, but she has worked, and continues to work, in these forms also. Her vitality and love and reverence for life show in all her work. That she is tough-minded and able to court sentiment while seldom becoming sentimental are bonuses. I hope you enjoy her work.

Harold M. Grutzmacher

REFLECTIONS

My Immigrant Heritage

Pride is a funny thing. Although we are in no way responsible for our ancestors we can be very proud of them, and grateful that because of them we were born Americans.

At some time all Americans were immigrants, coming to the New World to settle in a nation whose founders declared all men created equal and endowed by their Creator with the inalienable rights to life, liberty, and the pursuit of happiness.

And in this pursuit our ancestors came, some early, some late. As myriad drops of water gather to form rivulets, streams, rivers, lakes, and then the mighty ocean, so our ancestors' course joined that of other immigrants, and generations of Americans were born.

More than two hundred years ago one of my ancestors, David McKinley, emigrated to this country. He was born in 1755, in Scotland. During the American Revolution he served in Captain Joseph Reed's company.

After the war, he moved to Crawford County, Ohio, then part of the Northwest Territory, and died in 1840. David and his Scottish wife had two sons, William, who was born in 1807, and who was to become the father of President William McKinley, and James, born in 1783, who was my great-great-grandfather.

James settled in York County, Pennsylvania. His son, Peter McKinley, married Ellen Vossburg, who was born in 1819, in Canada. Peter and Ellen lived in Fairport, Ohio, but when Peter's business partner got into financial difficulties, they split the partnership and in settlement Peter got a trading post at Beaver Island, Michigan.

With Ellen and their three daughters, Sarah, 10, Effie, 8, and Mary, 5, they came to beautiful Beaver Island by sailing vessel in 1848. It had a lovely harbor, much fine timber and beautiful scenery. Fishing here was the best, and the island abounded in game.

Many tribes of Indians lived on Beaver Island, including Chippewas, who became friendly with the white people on the island and traded furs for supplies and food. The Indians also earned money during the summer and fall gathering wild strawberries, raspberries, huckleberries and cranberries. They were paid one dollar for a wooden pail full. A cooper on the island made the pails as well as barrels in which fish was shipped on the sailing vessels. Beaver Island was a place of much activity.

The Indian children were friendly with the whites, teaching them their games and bringing the girls bouquets of wild flowers, which they handed over on the points of their spears. They were very adept at fishing with these spears; standing upright in their birch bark canoes, they flashed the spears through the water and came up with fish every time.

The young Indians showed their fondness for the three girls, especially to Effie, whose red-gold ringlets fascinated them. Mary, the youngest girl, was terrified of some of the Indians, especially when they dressed in warrior style, and she would scream when she heard them coming. Sarah kept a record of life on the island, and she wrote that these were the happiest years of their lives.

Indian women were very proficient at bead work. Their moccasins were trimmed with beautiful patterned beading, and they used porcupine quills dyed with natural barks and roots to decorate their clothing.

There were many beautiful Indian women, some of whom carried papooses on their backs. Sarah says she could not recall ever hearing an Indian baby cry. The women had sweet, musical voices and were very neat in keeping their wigwams. They made lovely woven mats for the floors. The squaws did the heavy work, including all of the lugging for the braves. The Chippewa chief, Peaine, was devoted to Peter McKinley and his family and saved their lives in later years.

In the summer, steamboats brought mail to Beaver Island about every two weeks, and in winter French traders or half-breeds brought mail from the mainland over the ice with dog-teams. The islanders stocked up with supplies for the winter before navigation closed.

This pleasant life was not to last, for terror and violence came to the island. In 1849, James Jesse Strang brought a small colony of Mormons to Beaver Island, established himself as "King" and proceeded to take over. The group was a renegade offshoot of the followers of Joseph Smith, the original Mormon Prophet. Strang, a lawyer, brought many converts from outlying territories to the island. He acquired four wives, and his elders and apostles did likewise.

While on Beaver Island, Strang's flock pillaged the homes and property of the earlier settlers, stole fish ready for shipping, murdered some inhabitants, and drover others away. Peter McKinley stayed on (to protect his property) as long as he dared. His wife took the girls back to Ohio so they could attend school there.

Sarah McKinley records how Chief Peaine's brothers, Wa-ton-a-saw and Anden-e-mx, came to stay with Peter for two weeks to protect the family, and before leaving had a conference with Strang and his men. She recalls that the Mormons were told that all dealings with her father had been conducted in honesty, and that "if a hair on his head was injured by this outlaw Mormon band, the Indians would come and extermine them from the face of the earth." Peace reigned temporarily, but then worse depredations began and eventually Peter McKinley left the Island.

In 1856, Strang was shot by two of his own men. He was taken back to Voree, in Walworth County, Wisconsin, where his first and legal wife cared for him until he died. The Mormon colony was later driven off Beaver Island, but by that time, Peter and his family had settled on Mackinac Island.

While the family lived on Mackinac Island, Peter McKinley served two terms in the Michigan legislature at Lansing. Then, in 1854, an outbreak of cholera took the life of Ellen McKinley. Shortly thereafter, Peter and his daughters returned to Beaver Island. They found that only two apple trees stood where their house had been.

In 1859, Peter was appointed keeper of the lighthouse that had been built on Beaver Island. A year later, however, he became paralyzed, and his daughters Effie and Mary kept the light for nine years.

All three of Peter and Ellen's daughters married. Sarah married Herbert Livingston and moved to St. Louis. Effie and her husband, Capt. Nathaniel Kirtland, settled in Egg Harbor, Wisconsin. The youngest girl, Mary, met James Elworth Keith, a soldier who had marched with Sherman's Army and who was then stationed at Fort Mackinac. He had been born in Manchester, Iowa, on March 18, 1846, and they were married in Iowa on April 27, 1868. From this union two children were born — my father, Burton James Keith, in Guthrie, Iowa, July 17, 1869, and Grace Adele Keith, in Egg Harbor, Wisconsin, December 25, 1873.

When Burt Keith was about six, he went to live with his Aunt Effie and Uncle Nathaniel Kirtland. Their home was high on the Egg Harbor hill, overlooking the dock, where, when Burt was twelve, he started to help load cordwood for the steamboats. By the time he was nineteen, he had been sailing for some years and was the youngest sailboat captain on the lakes. One day he went over to Jacksonport to attend a program at the Temperance Hall, and there he met Mary Tollerton (Tollie) Bagnall, and a romance was begun.

Tollie was the oldest child of John Tollerton Bagnall, a timber cruiser in and around Jacksonport. A timber cruiser's job was to mark trees for the lumbermen to cut. John had been born in Canada, August 6, 1839, the fifth child of George Bagnall, who had emigrated to Frampton, Quebec, from Dunleary, Ireland, in 1835.

In the early 1860's, John left Canada for the States. In Chicago, after being robbed of his money and his gold watch, he got a job as a roustabout on a Goodrich boat going to Bailey's Harbor. From there, he walked to Jacksonport, where some Canadians he knew were working.

In 1869, John went back to Canada for a visit and returned to Jacksonport in January of 1870, with a bride, Eliza Rutherford. She had been born in the town of Armagh, in Ireland, and when she was five years old, her parents brought her to St. Malachie, Canada. In later years she told of that long crossing of six weeks by sail.

When Eliza married John Bagnall, she wore a purple wedding dress, in a custom known as "second mourning," because her mother had died only six months before. A true pioneer life was their lot. They moved about often because of John's work, living in log cabins chinked with moss. They got along with primitive means of cooking and hand made furniture, but they didn't miss the niceties of a more settled existence because no one else had them. There were few neighbors and many wild animals about, so game was readily obtained. Berries grew wild and those that they didn't eat fresh or in pies, Eliza preserved in stone jars sealed with a clean cloth dipped in wax. Using a dug-out canoe, they paddled up Logan's creek each night to get water for cooking and washing. A spring provided their drinking water. Wooden pails and tubs were made by a cooper who lived nearby. Each time they moved, a new camp had to be set up. Eliza did the cooking for the lumbermen. When they lived in log cabins Eliza whitewashed the walls and added homey touches by making frames for pictures and decorating shelves and boxes with spruce cones, which were plentiful. She made patchwork quilts, knit socks, and mittens of yarn she spun from fleece she had bought from farmers. She dyed the yarn with colors obtained from barks, berries, and onion skins.

There was no doctor or midwife in the village, so in October of 1870, a month before her first baby was due, Eliza walked to Sturgeon Bay, a distance of about 15 miles, to be near the assistance she would need. John followed shortly after with an oxen team bringing their belongings. She could not possibly have ridden in an ox-cart in her condition.

Halfway to Sturgeon Bay, Eliza stopped to rest at the Ash home, just east of where the Valmy church stands today. She was given a cup of tea, and Mrs. Ash sent her 17-year-old daughter to "walk a piece" with her and carry her bundle.

Three weeks after her baby was born, Eliza walked over to the shoe-maker's to be measured for a pair of shoes. She had very small feet, of which she was very proud, as she also was of her small wrists and ankles, a sign, she said, of "good breeding." Perhaps as a result of her early outing, she caught cold in her breasts, and Dr. Mac Eachem had to be called to treat her 18 times. Finally her breasts had to be lanced, and when she recovered and returned to Jacksonport, she was unable to nurse the baby. Every second day, teamsters brought milk over from Egg Harbor,where someone had a cow, until spring, when they found a farmer in Bailey's Harbor who had a cow. Thereafter John walked over every day for fresh milk. With no refrigeration, the only cold place they had to keep it was down in the well.

The young parents decided to move to where milk was more readily available, and in the fall, when Tollie was nearly a year old, they crossed Green Bay to Peshtigo, where John was able to continue working as a timber cruiser. But they had been there only a short time when the terrible fire of October 8, 1871, broke out — the same night as the Great Fire in Chicago. John and Eliza's house in what was called the "Sugar Bush country" was spared, but the holocaust was horrifying. John helped pick up the charred remains of the fire's victims; he built rough wooden coffins for those who were identifiable and helped bury the others in a mass grave.

My grandfather felt he couldn't bear to live among the memories of those terrible sights, so he and Eliza and little Tollie moved back to Jacksonport. Eight other children were born to them over the years, seven of whom lived: Mary, Harry, Rutherford, Samuel, Truman, Nellie, and Eva. Around 1880, John built a new home facing the road on the route past the lake. That house still stands, although much altered.

John, a dark-bearded man whose friends nicknamed him Black Jack, continued to work in the lumber woods. Eliza was known as a fine cook and a good neighbor; she was always available when there was sickness or sorrow in the village families. Reports from friends of the family described her as a hard-working woman, a Presbyterian by faith, straight-laced and proud, yet compassionate. As children, we heard a lot about her energy and industry. Mother told of her hemstitching the sheets she used to put on the lumberjacks' beds. She also had her light moments and often told her friends' fortunes with the tea leaves in their cups. Most indicative of her nature, I think, was the fact that when in later years she was given one of the new-fangled sewing machines that had a bobbin winder on it, she couldn't bear to waste the few minutes while the thread was being wound, so she would take up her knitting and "knit two, purl two" as she pedaled the machine.

John died in 1897, and his son,, Harry, died only two years later. Samuel and Truman worked farms in Jacksonport, while Rutherford ran a store in Cedarville, Michigan, and later on, moved to Sault Ste. Marie. My Mother, Mary (Tollie), taught school in Nasewaupee, then married, and lived in Jacksonport, Egg Harbor, and Sturgeon Bay. The other two girls, Nellie and Eva, lived at home until Eliza died in 1903; they then went to Milwaukee and learned the milliner's trade.

Tollie Bagnall and Burt Keith were married at Maple Ridge, Michigan, on January 30, 1893. After the ceremony they crossed the bay on the ice, with blankets and soapstones to keep them warm, but the wind sharp and stinging. As they neared Egg Harbor, every whistle in the town began to blow in welcome. Burt worked at Thorpe's store until it burned down, then at Washburn's Sawyer store, and when the Bank of Sturgeon Bay established a branch at Sawyer, he served as manager for 40 years. He also managed to study business at Valparaiso University.

The Burt Keiths had four daughters: Vera born in 1900, Verna in 1902, Grace in 1904 and Marian in 1910. Burt died in 1949, Tollie in 1955 at almost 85. The girls' marriages brought new nationalities into the family — Vera, Verna, and Grace married Norwegians, Marian a man of Bohemian and Scottish extraction. And their children found mates of such varied extraction that they proved the truth of the melting pot image of Wisconsin and of America.

My husband Stanley's family harks back to Samuel Swenson, born in Christiania, Norway, 1780. He died in Norway in 1850. His wife, Johanna Swenson, born 1796, died in Sturgeon Bay in 1880, having come here with her son, Sven Anton Samuelson in 1854. Although Sven and his wife, Hannah, had both been born in Norway, they met in America and were married in Manitowoc in 1864.

Sven was Liberty town clerk for 11 years. Although there were many other Norwegians who settled in that part of Wisconsin, few could read or write English. Sven had learned the language before coming to this country, and one of his practice books shows his diligent efforts at improving his writing ability and his penmanship. He served with Colonel Heg's 15th Wisconsin Infantry during the Civil War, participated in battles in Perryville and Chattanooga, and was commissioned a second lieutenant. In 1871 he became an assemblyman from Manitowoc county. Then, two years later, the family moved to Sturgeon Bay where many other Norwegians had settled. Sven bought 80 acres of farmland south of the bay on the Clay Banks road. Hannah gave birth to seven girls and five boys, including Albert Samuel, born in 1869, who was Stanley's father. Sven died in 1891; Hannah lived until 1929.

Albert Samuelson farmed and worked in the lumber woods as a youth, then was in the lighthouse service near Chicago. During the World's Columbian Exposition in Chicago in 1893, he conducted a lighthouse exhibit. Later he operated a restaurant in Chicago for 22 years. Albert married Hilma Theodora (Dora) Thompson in 1900, and they had eight children. For a while, Albert worked at the hay business, after which he operated a cherry and apple orchard for many years. He was a trustee of the Moravian church and served as a Sturgeon Bay alderman for 20 years. He died in 1944.

Albert's wife, Dora, who also came of Norwegian stock, was a member of the Helle family. Stefan Olsen Helle and his brother Ole Helle had made their first trip across the Atlantic in 1846. They went to Milwaukee first, then up to Port Washington and on to Cato and Manitowoc townships, where they looked for land that reminded them of their native Norway. Stefan was the first Norwegian to buy land in the county, and he built the first log cabin there. It took him two years to build, because it was all handcrafted. Two-way dove-tailed corners held the building together without nails, and the logs were fitted so perfectly that no mortar was required. It was a two-story cabin, intended to be a fine new home in a new land.

In 1847, several Norwegian families who had known Ole and Stefan in Valdres, Norway, came to America and settled nearby. Then, in 1848, Stefan returned to Norway and told everyone about the wonderful opportunities in America. He brought back with him about 15 families who settled in the new Valders. By this time, there was a sizeable settlement there, and Stefan was eager for it to grow more.

So, in 1852, he made another trip back to Norway. This time he returned with his mother and his fiancee, Marit Nildsdtr Fylken. On Lake Erie, their ship, the Atlantic, was rammed by the Ogdensburg. More than half of the 134 Valders recruits were drowned, including Stefan's mother, as well as 300 other immigrants. The Ogdensburg had gone on, but it returned and picked up as many survivors as possible. When they arrived in Wisconsin, Stefan and Marit were married by Pastor J. A. Ottoson, and later Stefan became an American citizen. To many people Stefan Olsen Helle was known as Stefan "Kubakke" after the name of the farm in Norway where he had lived.

Born at Vang, Norway, in 1818, Stefan was the son of Thomasen Shrebergeb. He fulfilled his military service in Oslo, and when he returned to Vang, he worked as a carpenter with Thomas Veblen. He was 34 years old when he and Marit settled in Valders, Wisconsin. At first he did carpenter work, helping others build their homes. Then, in 1861, he started a mill at Cato. He had previously tried a mill run by wind-power, but this wasn't practical. The mill at Cato was run by water-power. The first water mill he built was washed out when the dam give way but he rebuilt. Later he built a woolen mill at Cato, where they did spinning and weaving. After some years this mill was moved to Appleton, where Stefan's son took over the business.

This was beautiful country, with huge trees and productive soil, but building roads for the oxen and ox carts wasn't an easy matter. Where there were swamps, log poles were laid close together, making what were called corduroy roads. The Green Bay Way went north and east; the River Way followed the Manitowoc River, through Rapids and Rockland. Calumet Way went through Liberty and Eaton.

Six children were born to Stefan and Marit: Ole, Edwin, Thomas, Knute, Sarah, and Mary. The farm, where the first log cabin in Valders was built, passed on to Thomas. He became known as Tom's son, and according to Norwegian custom, the other boys were known as Ole—Tom's son; Knute—Tom's son, and Edwin—Tom's son, thus originating the surname Thompson.

When Thomas Thompson died, the farm passed into his estate, and several people farmed it. A frame house was built, and when Gordon and Olivia Thompson Helegsen lived there my husband and two girls and I visited them on several occasions. Olivia was my husband's cousin. One afternoon, I remember, we went out into the log cabin, which was used then for storage of wood and other things, and I found a stone jug about six inches in height, and with a capacity of 1 1/2 cups liquid. It had a brown glazed finish, and stamped near the bottom were the words, "D. L. Ormsby, 1848." Most likely it was used as a wine bottle, for there were corks still wired on. I am pleased to have a cherished memento from the first log cabin in Valders, Wisconsin. In 1974 the cabin was dismantled and moved to the Heritage Park historical village site in Manitowoc County.

Dora Thompson's grandfather, Thomas Olson Helle, was born in 1819. He married Kari Olson and they had six children. Their son, Ole Thompson Helle, who dropped the Helle name, was born in 1841. He married Olive Thiedemanson, and they had nine children. Two years after Olive died in 1880, Ole married Ida Kristianson. Hilma Theodora (Dora), the youngest child of his first marriage, grew up in Valders, and followed her older sisters, Galena, Emma, Matilda, and Clara to Chicago, when she was old enough to "work out." For the most part they went to various homes to do sewing. Their work was beautiful, with Dora doing most of the finishing on the tucked, embroidered, and stay-fitted dresses. Then, in 1900, Dora married Albert Samuelson. They had four boys, the oldest one of whom, Stanley, I married.

We are proud of our heritage, proud of the pioneer stock from which we came. Our own family has spread out from coast to coast, and our children's children have already seen much of this wonderful land of opportunity, the land that called out to our ancestors so many years ago.

Great-Grandma Was A Scientist

There's much emphasis these days on the scientific — on scientific farming, gardening, manufacturing, recreation, dieting, and homemaking. Great-grandma was a scientist, too, in her way. At least, she had her own scientific way of handling things, without scientific equipment.

Take cooking and baking, for example — chores that occupied three-fourths of her waking hours. She had no fat, candy, or meat thermometers, but instinct told her how to test for completion. If the cube of bread she dropped into her iron kettle of hot lard browned quickly, she would move the kettle to the spot on the stove-top where the heat stayed even, and start sliding in her fried cakes. A steady hand and a sharp eye registered when the syrup for divinity or boiled frosting spun a fragile thread as a few drops were poured from a spoon. And an oven was just right for starting a roast if she could hold her hand inside for just a moment. To put the meat in a cold oven was to make it lose its juices, with the result being a tough, tasteless roast. On the other hand, an "afternoon" oven was one that allowed you to hold your hand inside while you counted to ten. Oven heat was regulated by adding chunks of coal or wood and by opening or shutting the drafts to allow the fire to burn rapidly or slowly.

Certain rules held, too, during baking. Woe to the youngsters who banged the kitchen door or opened the oven door while her cake was baking. (Of course, some crafty boys weren't above doing it deliberately, because when a cake fell, she would pile on extra frosting, to cover the deficiency.)

There were many "scientific" tests that Great-grandma employed. She tested cake with a broom-straw or touched it with her finger to see if it sprang back; or she looked to see if it had shrunk from the edges of the pan, and she listened to hear if it had stopped "singing." Great-grandma often told of the hired girl, who, when asked if she'd seen that the knife came out clean when she tried it in the baked custard, replied, "Yes, and it worked so good that I cleaned all the breakfast knives that way."

Her test for a hot griddle was to see if drops of water bounced off its surface, and she gauged the heat of her sad-iron by touching it with the tip of a wet finger. (She wet her finger and held that out in the open air to tell which way the wind was blowing, too.)

She knew just how to test the liquid for yeast doughs on her wrist, and the baby's bath water with her elbow. She used tincture of benzoin to soften water for washing-up when the supply of rain water ran out in the cistern.

She kept eggs from August to spring (while the hens weren't laying) with quick lime and salt slaked with boiling water. And, along with almost everyone else, she stored barrels of apples, potatoes, carrots and rutabagas over winter to supply much-needed vitamins (though she had never heard the word). In spring, sulphur and molasses were doled out as a tonic, and dandelions provided the earliest fresh greens.

Perhaps it was instinct or folk wisdom, rather than science, that taught her what to do in emergencies: opening a puff-ball to stanch a flow of blood; putting mud or soda packs on a bee-sting; using onion poultices for chest colds and flaxseed poultices for boils. Goose-grease or mutton tallow mixed with gum camphor were other common chest rubs, and many a dose of the despised castor oil, epsom salts, and senna leaves she doled out. Wisely she stored jugs of boiled water in the storm shed for use during epidemics.

Great-grandma had her own recipes for beauty aids, too, including shampoo and cold cream. A "scruple" of sulphate of alumina added to a half pint of pure water and used on the face three times a day would eradicate wrinkles. And black tea made an excellent preparation to cover the gray.

Yes, in these and many other ways it was clear that Great-grandma had a storehouse of "science" at her fingertips, and she made good use of it.

She Left Me A Legacy

Mother had little of worldly goods, yet she left us a wealth of memories and treasures. Although I cherish her gifts to me (her mother's spinning wheel, coffee grinder, sad irons, silver caster, oil lamp, sherbet cups, and needlepoint friendship gifts), most of all I value her tattered Bible, a King James version with worn and shabby covers. It was probably about the fourth Bible Mother wore out, for she always read at least a chapter a day and marked favorite verses, notes, and comments.

But I treasure the volume all the more, for between those well-thumbed pages were crammed little slips of paper, clippings, poems, memo sheets, my father's obituary, old snap shots, a pressed flower or two—a veritable scrap book, symbols of her faith, her real character, her charitable thoughts. And believe, me, she was a woman to remember.

How often those little slips of paper have come to my aid for reassurance, for reference, for guidance, for use in Sunday School and Women's Society devotions, and for just plain daily living. On one scrap is written her favorite verse, from Timothy 1: 7; "For God hath not given us the spirit of fear, but of power, and of love, and of a sound mind." She lived to be 84, and how often I remember hearing her say she hoped she'd never be a burden to anyone, but would keep all her faculties to the last. She did, reflecting love, and the power of faith.

On another scrap was written the "Serenity Prayer," now used as a watchword for Alcoholics Anonymous, "God grant me the serenity to accept the things I cannot change, the courage to change the things I can, and the wisdom to know the difference."

There is a gift bookmark, in Scandinavian colors, from the friend of one of her daughters, congratulating her on her eightieth birthday and acknowledging her alertness and her contributions to community life. A newspaper clipping describes General MacArthur's plane, and there is a copy of Lincoln's Gettysburg address. Preserved here also are a Creed for

Happiness, given her by her sister-in-law, and her favorite poem, "Let me live in a house by the side of the road, And be a friend to man." All of these testify to her beliefs, as does a ragged clipping of a verse she learned long before her teaching days, "Still sits the schoolhouse by the road, A ragged beggar sunning."

More memory verses that strengthened her days are included. One square of paper listed two Bible verses, with her brother's name at the bottom, this her special message to him as he went through tragedy. Mother was a worry-wart, and she struggled always to overcome the tendency. So, a rag-taggle line on a scrap of blue stationery showed her faith crystal-clear: Jean McLaird's quote, "The degree of your anxiety, fear and worry is the measure of your distance from God." I'm sure she was very close.

Mother was a marvelous cook and baker, all the more so as she could never afford to be lavish with materials. But her fame spread in the locality. At Ladies' Aids or pot-lucks, folks looked for her feather-light biscuits, identified by the glossy tops and fork pricks. It was evident that she enjoyed these tasks. I found many favorite recipes not only written in her oil-cloth covered cook book, but slipped between the pages of the Psalms, along with little memos to herself written on days she was expecting visitors: "Mix bread. Make a cake. Cook potatoes with their jackets on. Get a trout or whitefish. Fix beet pickles and relish. Carrots and peas." As I read the items I can hear her tell the company, "Now, make out your dinner."

Like a jigsaw puzzle that, when put together, discloses a complete scene, so the messages on those scraps of paper from her Bible interlock to form a picture of her life. The list of names of 48 states and their capitals, which she recounted over and over to combat insomnia. (Sometimes she recited the names of the presidents.) When she was a little girl in school they learned by rote, and this habit carried through her life.

And the little slips of paper show her broad interests. History comes first, especially family history. On a single page of tablet paper, dogeared and well worn, is a very complete account of the Keith heritage. Years later, as I try to assemble our family trees, her record is indispensable. She included such things as advice from her father: "A wise woman reflects before she speaks. A foolish one speaks and then reflects on what she has uttered." "Modesty highly adorns a woman." The date was April 29, 1888. She was 18 then.

One note tells of her killing a five-foot pine snake with a cedar post

15

on her way home from school in her teaching days. An article from *Country Gentleman* reminds me of her wild flower garden on the east side of our home, the Sweet Mary that grew beside the woodshed, and her beautiful morning glories and forget-me-nots.

At a mother-daughter banquet one year she was asked to recall pioneer days. Her "speech" was written on a recipe card, which I found tucked between the pages of Matthew. I remember she dressed as a pioneer woman, and I recall, too, with shame, how we sometimes wished she'd stop talking about "old times."

Included too are some "flowers for the living," old letters that tell how much we appreciated her loving care and guidance, and thank you notes from old friends for tiding them over rough spots. Her charitable deeds didn't need to be recorded—they were remembered.

When on a warm June night she left us for an eternal home, she could take nothing with her. But she left behind a legacy; those tattered bits of paper that were the record of her life—a treasure-trove of dreams and memories. One could not ask for a more valued inheritance.

"My Father Says . . . "

"I tried to tell him it wouldn't work, but he doesn't listen. You might just as well go out and talk to the pump." That was my father talking, and I, a youngster of seven, had an image of my father going out in the back yard and having a conversation with the black contraption that furnished us water for the house. We four daughters took Dad's words literally, and he surely had a picturesque way of putting things.

He had no use for dishonesty, in businesses or in people. Many times I heard him dismiss a man's integrity with "You can't trust him any further than you can throw a bull by the tail." Of a hypocrite, he said, "That pirate! Sits in the front row in church every Sunday, and spends the rest of the week trying to beat folks out of their last dime." One man in particular roused his ire. Of him he said, "They ought to install a swivel chair for that fellow, so he could turn easier to see everyone who comes into church."

When we were bragging to our friends we were sometimes hampered by not being able to quote what father said. He considered much of what happened in his job as bank manager as confidential. While he might relate some incident or business deal at home, we were always cautioned, "Now don't you ever repeat this. Don't tell a soul." So, to this day, if I'm tempted to repeat a rumor I've heard, I imagine his finger pointing at me, and I'm too awed to spread the tale.

It was his manner of expressing himself that impressed us so. He didn't criticize the fellow who really wasn't very bright, but he was sharp in judgment of the one who didn't use his head. "Phew!" he'd exclaim, "that guy couldn't pound sand in a rat hole!" Or, "He couldn't make up his mind to come in out of the rain."

Most of his expressions probably stemmed from his nautical background. He was a sail boat captain on the lakes when he was nineteen. When things were in a sorry state, he might tell you, "There'll be the devil to pay, and no pitch hot." When we girls nagged him to allow us to do something unusual and tried to use the argument that everyone else could do it, he'd say, "Because everyone else jumps in the lake, do you have to?" he would come home sometimes and say, "We're in for a nor'easter. The storm flags are flying by the bridge today." (I wish I'd learned to read those flags as he did.)

He had no time for snobbery. If we set ourselves above someone he'd tell us, "Watch out for that Cod-fish aristocracy," referring to an eastern ancestor who had loved to play the grand lady. "Girls," he would lecture, "you can talk to everybody. You're just as good, but don't set yourself up as any better. Remember, your good name is the best thing you can own."

He had a passion for physical fitness. For many years he walked or bicycled across the bridge, to and from work. He put up a punching bag in the downstairs bedroom, and taught us how to shadow-box. And we got plenty of exercise, pushing the hand mower over our big yard. He never promised us pay, but when he came home to find the grass mowed, he'd say, "Well, now, I think a little girl deserves something for a good job like that." and would give us a coin as reward. For a while he was much impressed with Fletcherism, and we four girls would sit at the dining room table, chewing each mouthful of food 32 times, in rhythmic unison. (At least it kept us from arguing!)

A strict disciplinarian, he was, nevertheless, a sentimental softie. When I'd climb on his knee to be bounced a little, he'd assert, "You're the sweetest little girl who ever came over the Peakie-pikie-poke." That stemmed from a contrivance at the World's Fair called "Going over the Pike." Normally he was a very serious man, but I remember once seeing him do an Irish jig just for our amusement.

He made us wear long winter underwear till memorial Day, for fear we'd get chilled; and with his canvas-sail needle, he fashioned chamois skin vests to wear under our winter coats. We were cautioned interminably: "Don't go in a boat unless I'm along." "Don't go swimming in the Bay." "Don't go out without your rubbers." Don't, don't, don't. But we lived through the coddling and grew up healthy.

He had a well-developed instinct for diplomacy; though he might sputter at home about some injustice, he seldom argued with people. Once, however, he did get rip-roaring mad at work and hollered so loud they had to shut the windows. When he repeated how he'd "told them off," Mother asked, "What did they say?" "What could they say?" he countered.

Sometimes he'd tell us, "When a fellow's raising a family, he has to take a lot of guff. You might as well swallow your spit." Or, if he decided to take a chance on something he'd declare, "Might as well take the bull by the horns."

Where he got the expression, "The little monkey blows on his hands to get them warm, then blows on his food to make it cool," I'll never know. On first seeing a straw hat I bought one Easter, he told me it looked "like a cow chewed a chunk out of the back." He made up stories to tell my little sister about "Mamie-go-on in the North Woods." He loved to hunt, and we loved to see him come home from hunting. Then we went through his jacket to see if we could find any of the German's Sweet Chocolate or raisins he always carried, in case he lost his way. Sometimes when he'd read our local newspaper, the *Door County Advocate*, he'd make up items and pretend he was reading them from the paper. This was hilarious to us, as he was ordinarily so serious.

When Mother walked out with guests who were leaving, sometimes going as far as the car, he'd say, "Why didn't you take them out to the Fair Grounds?" One evening Mother mused, "I don't know whether I should go over and visit with Mrs. Johnson tonight, or stay home and iron," Dad spoke up, "Oh, I think you'd better stay home and iron." (He seldom went anywhere at night, and was usually in bed by 8:30.) He did take us to boat launchings, and we all went along for picnics whenever he steered a friend's gasoline launch up and down Green Bay. But we weren't allowed to go to Sunday movies.

Life with Father was never monotonous. He occupied spare moments with Scouting, camping, and hunting; he trained in the National Guard in World War I; and he was a history buff. When his pessimistic tendencies got the better of him, he'd say "We're going to land in the Poor House." But Mother always topped this with: "You may go, but I'm not going there with you!"

Father Of The Groom

"I'd have fired a waiter who cut bread like that!" Looking at the loaf of home-made bread that, in my inexperience, I had managed to slice on the bias, I laughed. That was the most severe criticism my father-in-law ever gave me. Years before he had operated a restaurant in Chicago, and though he had come back to the old homestead to grow cherries, we often heard of his restaurant experiences.

It seems to me they should celebrate a special day for fathers-in-law. From the time he becomes the father of the groom to his rocking-chair days, he's generally the one much more tolerant and appreciative of the daughter-in-law's efforts and attitudes, the one more ready to accept her into the family.

Aside from the fact that this special man was the father of my special man, there were many wonderful things about him. Was it, I wonder, because of the many thoughtful things he did for me, that I have such fond memories of him? He taught me the bird songs in the orchard, and around the old farmhouse. He made birdhouses out of pieces of hollow log, hung them throughout the orchard, and the bluebirds came back to those homes year after year. He showed me where to get the richest soil for my flower beds and houseplants and how deep to plant the seeds. He put up extra clothes lines for me, fixed a door that wasn't hung properly, got fine clean sand from a spot in the orchard for the girls' sand box. He carried extra pails of water in from the pump for me during the day, kept the coal scuttles and wood boxes filled when Stanley was at work, and shoveled a path to our outside bathroom facilities on blizzard days. Many a time he filled the tubs and wash boiler for me. He had a wonderful way with children. I can see him bouncing them on his knee, singing in Norwegian what sounded to my alien ears like, "Rea rea runkin, Hesta, hesta prunkin—" at the end of which he'd give a big bounce and call, "Woof, woof, woof!" while the children squealed in delight. When he came into the house and heard the baby crying, he'd go to the crib or play-pen, pick up the baby, and inquire, "Are they mean to you?" As a new mother, his question bothered me; I worried that he might really think I was being mean. I soon learned, however, that he just couldn't stand to hear a baby cry.

Never one to brag, he was capable of making or fixing almost anything. When I complained about the chickens getting into my flower beds, he fenced them around and covered the tops, too. For a while, he kept a cow and would come up from town every morning to care for her and milk her. He would bring the full pail into the kitchen to strain the milk and would give me all the milk we could use before taking the rest home.

One day when I was trying to persuade Stanley to do something my way, I remarked, "Your father would do it the way I wanted." To which he replied, "Oh, it's too bad you didn't marry my father instead of me!" Grandma loved that, and repeated it often.

He lived an interesting life. Son of a Civil War veteran of the battles of Perrysville and Chattanooga, he had once been a lighthouse keeper. From about 1890 through the early 1900's, he had operated an oyster house restaurant on Madison Street in Chicago. About 1908, he moved his family to Sturgeon Bay and built a house on Maple Avenue. He worked in the hay and feed business, cut wood in the swamp in winter, and sold seed gathered from cedar and other evergreens. Finally he bought the old homestead, 80 acres of land about a mile out of town, and planted a cherry orchard. For years the old farm house stood unoccupied, used for storage and for drying and sieving seeds spread out on floors upstairs. Then came the Depression, and with unemployment staring us in the face, Stanley and I moved into the house and fixed it up for habitation.

What a heritage he left us and his grandchildren—memories of a fine, upstanding man, a kindly soul. For more than 20 years he was a town councilman, and during the Depression, when he was in charge of the relief committee, people would line up at his home, seeking assistance. He handled their cases with compassion, asking nothing in return. Many times, however, I heard him say, "If you have any bouquets for me, give them while I'm living." He was a man of quiet religious faith who saw to it that his family got to church every Sunday, even when he had to pull the boys on a sled across the ice on the bay. When someone made a disparaging remark about church-going, he'd say, "Well, at least you won't learn anything bad there!"

His varied experiences made him an interesting conversationalist. He

21

enjoyed Western movies, and nothing was allowed to interfere with his schedule of radio listening. His favorites were "Amos and Andy" and "Death Valley Days."

He didn't care much about dressing up, often wearing disreputable looking sweaters and jackets. Many times, when we stopped at the house downtown to visit, we'd find him at the kitchen table, weaving yarn in and out of the gaping holes in his sweater elbows or wool socks. He enjoyed doing that, and he showed real appreciation for Grandma's beautiful efforts at quilt making and her lovely needlepoint.

Shortly after Stanley, the children, and I moved to Milwaukee in 1941, he began having heart trouble. During his last days, in 1944, I took the train up to see him in the hospital. He smiled when he saw me, and said, "You've come home!"

I can picture him, in that Home in the sky, singing to the littlest angels in his rumbling way, "Rea, rea, runkin. Woof, woof, woof!"

Dog And Pony Show

That summer of 1912, Mama and Papa took a two weeks' vacation. It was remarkable, as Papa had always felt that if he left the branch bank for more than a day or two things would get all balled up. He reminded us of the times he and Laura Fetzer had to stay real late because the balance was a few cents under or over. Laura's book keeping, Papa's records, and the amount in the cash drawers before it was carried into the big vault had to tally exactly. No computers then, and checks had to be filed and coins rolled by hand before the timer was set on the vault and the bank doors triple locked. But Mama had convinced him that he needed a change, and the president, Mr. Fetzer, had promised to send over his nephew to take his place temporarily. Plans were to go up to Mackinac Island on the Goodrich boat, to spend a couple of days there, and then visit Mama's brother and sister-in-law at Cedarville, on the Upper Michigan peninsula. Papa's grandmother was buried on Mackinac. He wanted to see her grave, and also Fort Mackinac, where his grandfather was stationed after the Civil War. He hoped to get to visit Beaver Island, where Grandma Keith grew up, and where her family were driven off by the Mormons, led by the infamous "King" Strang, who attempted to keep his followers in his power. I had heard Grandma tell about it many times.

They were taking the baby, Marian, who was two years old, along with them. We three girls were to be in Grandma's care. We looked forward to our freedom, and wondered what they'd bring back for us. Mama had been busy right up to the time she left for the boat getting our summer dresses ready and hung in the upstairs closet, our Sunday dresses over at one side. We got strict orders that our play, or everyday, dresses were to be worn two days, and that the embroidered whites would be good for two Sundays if we changed as soon as we got home from Sunday school. Then Grandma wouldn't have to get out the washboard, tubs, or boiler. Dresses and petticoats had to be starched and ironed with the sad irons heated on the old range. Vera and Verna could keep clean easily, but somehow I could never keep tidy looking. My clothes seemed to attract mud and dirt, grass stains, spots and wrinkles. My nose was usually skinned from falls, and stray curls always dripped from my blond braids.

Grandma was very deaf. She had a hearing aid, a cloth covered arm long tube with a hard rubber tube to insert in her ear, and a mouthpiece at the other end, like that on the telephone. The idea was for her to place the small tube in her good ear, then we'd shout into the mouthpiece. The sound was supposed to be amplified, but what one really heard was some muffled gibberish, so we disregarded the hearing aid and shouted in her ear. That way she could catch most of what we were saying. Grandma was very good at lip reading, so we had to watch our table language. I might think I had got away with some flippant remark, but Grandma's 'Why, Gracie Keith!" brought me back sharply. It would be sort of fun, we thought, to have a change of discipline; we planned to take advantage when we could.

The day they left for the trip we walked down to the Goodrich dock to see them off. Papa, in his best suit, his Panama hat with just the right crease, carried the heavy leather suitcase, and Mama pushed the baby in the folding stroller. We watched them board the big ship, all the time getting final instructions as to staying far back on the dock, and in going straight home afterward. The draw on the old bridge began to open as the bridge tender went round and round the turnstyle to open the draw. We waved our handkerchiefs as the boat wended her majestic way toward Green Bay waters. Then we started home—but not *straight* home; naturally we walked up town and stopped in at Washburn's store to spend some of our vacation spending money. It took a while to choose the candies from the big glass case. Mr. Cheeseman was patient as I chose a penny's worth of little mixed. Verna chose a dumbbell: that sweetwood stick covered with chocolate with bells of chocolate-covered taffy at each end. That would last a long time. Vera bought a maple sugar heart, and we each chipped in a penny to bring Grandma a bag of her favorite peppermints.

Grandma was waiting for us, and, if we thought we were going to get away with a lot, we soon learned that Grandma could delegate authority. We couldn't get away with as much as we thought. We knew better than to rebel—there would be reckoning when Papa and Mama got home. We did our chores without too much grumbling. Then we could hurry over to our friends' houses to wait until they were free to come out.

Some things we did get away with, like taking off our shoes and stockings to walk barefoot in puddles in the road after a rain (What bliss! Papa
had never allowed us to go barefoot; we might cut our feet.), climbing
up on the roof of the woodshed, bringing dolls out to the hammock. When
it rained the mud in the puddles made lovely frosting for our mud pies
and cakes. We coaxed Grandma to cook our favorite dishes, and quickly
used up the supply of cookies and doughnuts Mama had left stored in the
cellarway.

Grandma made gingerbread men for us, and we coaxed her to let us
make ice cream and popcorn and candy. She made pink lemonade for us,
too, squeezing the lemons, adding plenty of sugar, and putting the lemon
rinds into the glass pitcher that Verna filled up with cold water from the
pump. We couldn't use ice in it because Papa said the bay ice was full
of germs.

One thing Grandma excelled in was story telling. Both Mama and Papa
entertained us often with tales of their youth, and we loved those stories
of pioneer days. But Grandma told the wonderful old favorite stories that
were in our readers, and took the parts so realistically and dramatically
we shivered when the tigers in "Little Black Sambo" growled, and giggled
when Grandma's cracked voice made a perfect imitation of Epaminondas'
mother saying, "Epaminondas, what you got dere?" Grandma wasn't above
using the stories as a bribe if she wanted us in early from playing out after
supper. Sometimes the neighbor girls would come in to hear the fun.

That June the weather was stifling, so we didn't indulge in games that
were too active. We had tea-parties on the front porch, with cambric tea,
made with milk and hot water with a spoon of sugar, served with cookies
or crackers spread with honey. The thick Virginia creeper vine that grew
on the ell part of the porch shielded us from the hot afternoon sun, and
welcome breezes would waft through the leaves. It was a great time to read
our favorite books; the Oz books I brought from the library; *Girl of the
Limberlost*, *Lassie*, and *Little Women*. We often acted out our favorite
stories for neighborhood friends, or lolled lazily in the hammock, and sometimes laid on the grass and watched cloud pictures.

Evenings were best. The neighborhood children gathered for games at
the vacant lot on the corner. Grandma liked supper early and we did, too,
since it meant longer time for playing out after dishes were done. We poured
hot water from the teakettle into the enamel dish pan on the zinc-covered
work table, more into the rinse pan, scrubbed the dishcloth on the bar

of Fels Naphtha soap to make suds. I stood on a stool to reach the pan; Verna or Vera wiped the dishes I washed while the other swept the kitchen and put the "between meal cloth" on the table. Soon the air resounded with "Pum, pum-pullaway" "Auntie, auntie over!" or "Here come ten thousand men to work." Grandma sat in her rocker, shawl round her shoulders, and rocked and crocheted.

By the second week our freedom was paling a little. In the frenzy of "feeling our oats," we had stretched ourselves to the fullest. The two older girls seemed to be getting more bossy every day. I didn't dare complain to Grandma, knowing full well they would tattle on me; I was guilty of snitching sugar from the sugar bowl and sneaking extra treats. Grandma kept us all busy, picking and preparing vegetables from the garden, going down town on errands, sweeping porches and walks and doing all the regular chores. She could think of more things for us to do, especially if we were just about to slip off to a friend's house. On the second Thursday she told us, "You girls had better clean the yard and cut the grass today. You don't want your Papa coming home to find it looking like that." We moaned, but dragged out the old push mower and took turns shoving the heavy machine around, huffing and puffing, getting blisters on our hands from gripping the handle and on the spots where the big shears, used to trim edges of the lawn, rubbed the skin. It was hard work and we made slow progress.

Then suddenly a big canvas covered wagon, pulled by a team of huge work horses turned off the street and into the big vacant lot at the corner. Three other horse-drawn wagons followed. We left our yard work and ran over to see what was going on. Could it be the Chautauqua? No, that wasn't due for another week. Anyway the tent was always set up in Market Square. The lot wasn't big enough for a circus big-top; that usually was out at the Fairgrounds. The small circus that had come at the last of the summer a year ago was held on the lots behind the Hopp orchard. Crowding into the alley beside the Hutto place, we eyed the scene with growing curiosity. From all directions other boys and girls appeared, curious too.

Verna discovered what it was all about. "Look, there's a sign on the side of that wagon: HILLBRETH'S FAMOUS DOG AND PONY SHOW. It *is* a circus! Excitedly, we speculated on the arrival: how many animals they had, and the performers, and the price of admission.

Then we were struck with the awful truth. We had no money. We couldn't possibly go. All of the treat-money Papa had given us had disappeared the first week, on candy and gum, and the Saturday afternoon movie. Even Verna, who was the thrifty one, had only ten cents left. We wailed, thinking of Papa, always so generous in paying us for extra chores, who wasn't here to help us out. No use asking Grandma. Just yesterday she had said she had given her last dollar to the Bible salesman. Penny banks— no good. We had no key.

We envied the boys who had seized the opportunity to earn their way in to the show by helping put up the tent and doing errands for the crew who worked fast to get ready for the afternoon show. All of us neighborhood girls, watching, grieved. "Why couldn't we have been boys so we could earn admission tickets?" And we Keith girls added, "Why did Papa and Mama have to go away at a time like this?"

Then Grandma called us, her cracked voice telling us to come home and help get dinner ready. We tore ourselves away from the spot which was both fascinating and tragic. Dejectedly we set at our chores; Vera was peeling potatoes, I set the table, and Verna took the pail to refill with fresh water. She give a little squeal and rushed outside, banging the screen door behind her. Working the pumphandle with strong, even strokes, one of the roustabouts concentrated on filling water pails. Beside him one of the Minor boys waited to carry extra pails. He nodded pleasantly to Verna as he handed the overflowing pails to Morris.

"Wait!" Verna spoke briskly although her voice trembled a little. "This is our well. If you want to haul water for the animals you'll have to give us free passes. The well might go dry, you know, from pumping so much."

The man set down the pails as he turned to face her. "Sure, sister," he grinned. "How many do you need?"

I was peering out the window, while Vera shouted in Grandma's ear to explain what was going on. Verna bounced into the house to get to Grandma's good ear. "Do you want to go to the Dog and Pony Show?"

"Mercy, no. I can't hear any of it, anyway. And crowds make me nervous."

Verna careened out again and informed the man that we needed three passes. I followed the two and watched them water the ponies. Then he pointed to the ticket office, holding up three fingers to the fancy looking lady in the booth, who handed me three cardboard tickets. I skipped alongside the show man as he went back for more water; then I rushed inside to show the treasures. "You should *see* what I saw over there! I bet they have twenty ponies and fifty dogs! I saw the crew eating at a long table outside. They had stew. Do you suppose they eat the ponies? And I saw three beautiful ladies, in TIGHTS!"

Grandma, reading my lips, was horrified. "TIGHTS! That's no kind of a show for young girls to see! Your Papa would never let you go!"

We stared at her in horror. All this agony to get tickets and now she wouldn't let us go? The girls looked at me in disgust. Why did I spill that about the tights?

Vera, the diplomat, spoke up quickly. "Oh, I'm sure he would . . . Papa loves a circus."

Thus mollified, Grandma give in. We rushed through the meal preparation with no wrangling, and dishes were washed at top speed, the three of us singing in harmony. We washed up speedily and ran up to change into clean clothes. Another stumbling block. Our best ginghams and linens were all in the dirty clothes. There was nothing to do but wear our embroidered white Sunday dresses. That scared us a little; Mama would surely scold when she got back. We salved our consciences by tying on our second-best ribbon sashes. We wiped off our patent leather slippers with vaseline and gartered our long white stockings as tight as possible. There were the usual grass stains on my knees, but that had never bothered me.

Before she lay down to take a nap, Grandma braided my hair: so tight it seemed as if my eyes would pop out. I wore two long braids, hair curled around Grandma's finger below the rubber band halfway down. Vera and Verna tied their braids in cradles, and we all wore our very best watersilk hair ribbons. For once, I looked "slicked-up."

We walked down the alley and into the field where the show was being held. There was a bad moment at the office booth. Would the ticket-taker ask us for money, too? We held our breaths. The man in the booth barely glanced at the cardboards; just motioned for us to go in.

The long wooden bleachers were filling up. We found seats as quickly as possible, self-conscious in our Sunday finery. We leaned forward, not to miss a thing. The dogs and ponies went through their acts smartly and we marvelled at their tricks: leaping through blazing hoops, racing, playing dead, catching the balls. The sleek ponies were a joy to watch, too; as they went through their practiced show they seemed almost human. We girls agreed that the beautiful ladies astride the ponies, in their sparkling garb were not immodest hussies as Grandma had implied. We told each other that they couldn't possibly have jumped from horse to horse, or stood on their heads if they had worn dresses. Every second there was a new thrill. Wait till we could tell Papa about it! We looked around to see if anyone we knew was there.

The pink lemonade (made, no doubt, from our well water) looked inviting. But Verna used her last dime and bought a bag of popcorn, which we all shared. We made it last throughout the whole performance.

At last we straggled out, tired, worn, and happy, yet a little regretful. I had torn my good dress on a nail and fallen to my knees to leave deeper grass and dirt stains on my Sunday stockings. Verna looked as neat as a pin as she bent down to wipe a speck of dust from the patent leather slippers with her handkerchief. Vera's dress was unwrinkled; she had carefully lifted her skirt before she sat down.

Everything looked unfamiliar in the bright sunlight. We stood a minute, blinking, then stopped, aghast. At the corner of the lot, surveying the crowd coming out of the tent, were the neighbor Johnson girls. Vera touched my arm. "Oh" she grieved, WHY didn't we ask for six passes instead of three? They could have come then, too."

"Never mind," Verna grinned. Those animals will have to have more water; I'll tell them they have to give us three more passes." So they got there after all. And for weeks afterward the neighborhood kids put on "Dog and Pony Show." Every pet within six blocks was pressed into "entertaining."

There was still the piper to pay when Mama and Papa got home and saw the mountain of dirty clothes and heard Grandma's report. And, like Epaminondas, "I'm not going to tell you what happened." But maybe you can guess.

Black Cats And Sidewalk Cracks

G rowing up in the teen years of this century, our life-style was considerably different from that of young folks today. I remember how much more aware of superstitions we seemed to be. What has happened to them? People today may have their phobias, but you seldom hear of the influence of the signs, predictions, or premonitions that we commonly accepted back in those days. Oh, sure, we laughingly knock on wood, we avoid sitting 13 at a table, and we may still wish on the first star (just for the heck of it), but the old-time symbols, warnings, and forebodings seem to have gone with the passing years.

Back in pre-World War I days, we were definitely affected by such beliefs — they were part of our way of life. When you got up in the morning, you were careful to put your right foot out first, and to get out on the right side of bed. If you neglected that ritual, your whole day went wrong, and you were an old crab.

When you got dressed, should you accidentally put your underwear on wrong side out, you wore it that way all day for luck. And if you sang before breakfast, someone was sure to remind you that you'd cry before supper. Likewise, if a girl had the temerity to whistle, she was told: "A whistling girl and a crowing hen always come to some bad end."

When your cup of coffee had bubbles floating on the top, you hurried to capture them in your spoon before they reached the rim. Otherwise, you'd lose the "money" the bubbles indicated was coming your way. If you dropped a knife or fork, company was on its way. And if you accidentally buttered both sides of your bread, that was a sign that someone was coming hungry. (Probably also a sign that you'd get scolded for being extravagant.)

If all the food on the supper table was eaten, you could be sure the weather next day would be nice. If you spilled the salt, you were obliged to throw a pinch of it over your left shoulder to avoid a quarrel.

30

The worst kind of bad luck would follow for seven years should you be so unfortunate as to break a mirror. And you had always to be on the lookout to avoid stepping on a crack, for if you did, you'd break your mother's back. (Most mothers' backs were almost broken, anyway, from hours bending over the washboard and scrubbing hardwood floors on hands and knees.) You said "bread and butter" if you and your friend happened to walk on either side of a post, or if someone stepped between you.

Did your ear start ringing? If it was the left ear someone was saying something bad about you; if the right, that meant a good report. And if you happened to glimpse the new moon over your left shoulder, you quickly made a wish, and didn't tell anyone.

You wished when you blew out the candles on your birthday cake; if they all went out your wish would come true. I had a wish come true once when I found a four-leaf clover. My mother suggested that I put it in the Bible and wish for a baby. Sure enough—sure enough—within a short time, I had a little baby sister!

We must have gone around all day making wishes. We wished on loads of hay, we stamped our fists against our hands and wished when we saw a white horse, and we thrilled to get the long end of a wishbone, knowing that our wish would come true.

Omens ran rampant. Most were stated in verse, like: "Stub your toe, Meet you beau; Kiss your thumb, He's sure to come." "Homely in the cradle, pretty at the table." "Red sky at night, sailors' delight; Red sky at morning, sailors' warning." "Rain before seven, clear by eleven." Even sneezing had meaning: "Once, a wish; twice, a letter; three times a kiss; four something better." Weddings had many associated symbols: "Lucky is the bride the sun shines on." "Married in white, you've chosen all right. Married in blue, he'll always be true. Married in yellow, ashamed of your fellow. Married in green, ashamed to be seen. Married in red, you'll wish yourself dead." And, of course, "Something old, something new. Something borrowed, something blue."

In our strict household the only card games we were allowed to play were flinch, authors, old maid, and the like. But there was one game (was it fortunes?) with cards that pictured all kinds of good and bad signs and omens and correlated them with sayings such as, "Dream of a wedding, hear of a funeral" or "Good luck if you stumble going up stairs" or "Bad luck to kill a cricket."

Friday afternoons at school we had "literary meetings," where we acted out plays or recited "memory gems," which included adages, poems, etc. We were discouraged from reciting superstitious jingles, but I can remember one time when, for want of any other memory gem, I gave a verse that had been burned on a piece of tanned leather my folks had brought back from a vacation trip: "Worry not over the future, the present is all thou hast. The future will soon be the present, and the present will soon be the past." Despite that admonition, I've spent a lifetime worrying.

I can't recall that we ever had a horseshoe hanging over our door, but we knew that if we kept a penny in our shoe, we wouldn't go broke. And if we got a present of something sharp, like scissors or a knife, we made sure to hand the giver a penny to break the spell. A bird flying into your house was a bad luck omen. And if you told your dreams before breakfast, they would never come true.

Our parents must have been believers too. Our mothers knew that if you said thanks for a slip from a plant, it wouldn't grow. If you could swipe a slip without the owner seeing it, especially a slip with a bud, it would bloom for you better than the original.

Even dishwashing had its omens. If you were the kind who got the front of your dress wet while doing dishes, someone surely would tell you that you were going to have a drunken husband.

Just about all girls would put a piece of wedding cake under their pillow whenever the opportunity presented itself, so that their dreams would come true. We were wary of black cats crossing our paths and of walking under a ladder. If your nose itched you knew you were going to kiss a fool. Grandmothers warned: "Where cobwebs grow, no suitors go." And, with the limited opportunities women had in those days, it paid to sweep down the walls.!

Our acceptance of these and other superstitions may appear silly in these more sophisticated times, but like so much else from long ago, they were a part of a way of life that gave us all the security and comfort we needed to grow up and become the disdainers of superstitions we are today.

Birdie's Revenge

Before the outbreak of World War I, segregation was a word never heard in Sturgeon Bay. No one mentioned black power, and the various nationalities that made up the community were accepted as a matter of course. Our "foreigners" — the Chinese laundry man who did up the men's white shirts so beautifully, the Italian shoe-repair man with the marvelous singing voice, three or four Jewish families, the Hindu missionary who had visited the last revival meeting — these and more were accepted at face value. We didn't know what a minority group was, and for the most part, we grew up without prejudice.

So it was quite a shock to several of us in the seventh grade when prejudice exploded right in our midst. What is now the junior high building at that time housed both grade and high school. I remember our seventh grade classroom, located at the northeast corner of the second floor, and I remember the day my story concerns. Several of us girls were in the cloakroom, struggling to get into high-buckled overshoes, and to pull on coats, tam-o-shanters, and long woolen gauntlets. In the process, we were chattering a mile a minute discussing details of the social that we had been asked to plan.

Into this spirited group two of the boys in our class appeared, returning to pick up books they had forgotten and that would be needed for homework. We ignored them; our discussion was too interesting to be bothered with boys.

One of the boys, however, didn't ignore us. "What is this," he asked, "a Jewish picnic?"

It passed over most of our heads; but not Birdie's, whose family was Jewish. Quick as a flash her hand flew out and she struck him squarely on the mouth. Then, instinctively, she ran — to the girls' lavatory, where she was safe from retaliation. We all followed her, quickly. We knew the boy wasn't going to let a thing like that go by without getting even, but how were we going to get Birdie out of the building unnoticed?

One of our group had an inspiration. "Look," she said, "Dorothy looks a lot like Birdie. She has dark hair, wears glasses, too, and she's about the same size. Why don't we just exchange coats and caps, and then we can sneak Birdie out one door, and Dorothy out the other?"

With much giggling, this was done. Birdie's red coat and matching tam fit Dorothy perfectly, and Dorothy's brown coat looked right on Birdie. Both girls pulled their tams low on their foreheads and wrapped their woolen scarves around their faces, covering all but their eyes.

We consulted again, and decided that if the boys were watching for us, they would most likely be waiting outside the "girls' door." To be on the safe side, we checked — one girl going down to the girls' door, one to the boys' door, and one to the front door. When we gathered again, Lela reported that the villain was, sure enough, waiting for Birdie outside the girls' door, with a pile of snowballs at his side. And an accomplice was making an extra supply.

Cautiously, we separated; two girls going out each door. Birdie and Lela slipped out the boys' door; two of us left by the front door, and Dorothy and Eva came out the girls' door on a run. All of us were headed for Sibree's corner, where the Episcopal church now stands.

Four of us weren't intercepted at all. We made it to the corner and stood waiting. Dorothy, however, got only a few steps out the door when she was grabbed. With his fists full of snow, he lunged at her. But just before his hand connected with her face, Dotty yanked off her scarf and laughed at the look of frustration that came over him.

With a disappointed howl, he dashed around to the other door hoping to intercept the real Birdie, but, of course, he was too late. Birdie and her protectors had fled.

There, on the street, Dorothy and Birdie changed back into their own wraps. We were proud of our successful efforts, and we praised Birdie for putting something over on the boys. It never crossed our minds that we had also participated in an expression of protest against a thoughtless slur.

The Creek In Springtime

Every year, after the snow has been gone for about a month, I feel an uncontrollable urge to walk down to the creek. So, some sunny morning I set aside my tasks for a half-hour, and walk through the old family cemetery, down the rutted road that leads near the creek. I watch for early blooming flowers along the wayside, trilliums, spring beauties, and anemones. There are pools of water in the road; it won't drain completely off until June. I pass the old apple orchard—those trees will be bulldozed out this year, and we'll miss their bright blossoms and colorful fruit. A gravel pit will take over there.

Across the road from the orchard, however, is the creek, rippling and rushing along through the huge hardwoods and over fallen logs gowned in thick green moss. It meanders along a deep-cut channel, the large cedar, oak, maple, and clumps of birch reaching clawlike roots into the water. Sumac and witch hazel bushes cling to the sides of the stream. The grass and weeds grow lushly, even when the creek has dwindled to a trickle in hot weather. There are stepping stones to cross it in some places; in others, huge logs make convenient bridges. The water is shallow in spots, and under the big trees one finds deep pools reflecting the blue of the sky, and perhaps even sheltering a fish or two. Nestling under fallen leaves are clumps of purple and yellow violets; we always carry a bouquet home, even though they will not last more than a couple of days in water. Sometimes there are wintergreen berries, and, under the trees, the carpeting of moss is so thick and springy one hates to step on it.

Here are treasures—if you're a nature lover. Perhaps you find an old bird's nest, and you marvel at the expert way it was woven. A bird's colorful feather lies on the ground by an unusual fungus which you take along for a flower arrangement. Odd little colored pebbles, and sometimes some fossil rock intrigue you. You pick up a burled branch and see baby ferns unfurl their tiny emerald fronds. You splash your fingers through the cool, sun-dappled water, catching a little crab or tadpoles.

The colors are so restful: deep green of evergreens; chartreuse of budding leaves; pink blush of trillium and spring beauty; deep purple of violets, nestling close to brown tree trunks and framed in a mossy shadow box. These colors are framed by blue sky, and repeated in the clear stream, little clouds dimpling here and there. And the birds—thrushes and bob-o-links, warblers and wrens. Later we see the flash of orioles and gold-finches and bluebirds. We pause at a hummock, and stand enrapt while busy little ants bustle about their business, carrying loads many times heavier than they. Bees fly about, investigating the nectar of the flowers, and here and there a butterfly lights on a leaf, gently fanning its wings. Mosquitoes spawned in stagnant pools buzz around us; we brush them off impatiently.

Everywhere the fragrance of spring is evident—the spicy smell of cedar, the moist, pungent smell of the grass and moss underfoot, the delicate odor of the blossoms, even the alliaceous whiff of leek and skunk cabbage and the dank scent of decayed leaves and branches. I breathe deeply, savoring it all. Now, I must return to the heat of my stove, the prosaic beauty of prepared food, and the aroma of baking. But I'm refreshed.

Collectibles

Isn't it amazing how time changes our attitudes concerning even the most common objects? Today you consider yourself lucky to find — and be able to afford — a "collectible," which often is nothing more than an everyday household item of the past, an item that had been forgotten, given away, or thrown out because folks felt there was no further use for it now that "improvements" had come.

No use saving the old oil lamps or barn lanterns when electricity became available. Who cared to put up with the old coal or wood ranges with their coal scuttles and ashpans, when kerosene stoves — to say nothing of gas or electric ranges — came in?

Those old brass beds, feather mattresses, straw ticks, and commodes, as well as the water pitchers, basins and other paraphernalia that the commodes contained — banish 'em to the basement or the attic!

In the twenties, the craze was for color. Painted or lacquered furniture was favored everywhere. Layers of paint covered those priceless old rockers, dressers, drop-leaf tables, and kitchen chairs that in later years would require hours of stripping, sanding, and refinishing to restore them to their original handsome state.

If anyone had the good sense to save some of those old-time articles, many would be found to be as useful today as they were in the past, regardless of progress. I remember Mama's old black dripping pans that turned out much marvelous home-made bread, and the iron gem tins and muffin tins that bake as beautiful a variety of muffins today as they did a hundred years ago.

I couldn't bear to keep house without Mama's Dutch oven, and if I had her bread-raiser I'd enjoy using it today. She was very proud of her mother's coffee grinder, which I do have; I treasure it though now its use is purely ornamental. The old casters, with bottles for vinegar, oil, catsup, mustard, etc., were handy things to own. That spatterware water pail with the accompanying dipper could be put to many uses.

The soup pot, the canning kettle, the double boiler that cooked the breakfast oatmeal at the back of the coal stove overnight, they're all handy gadgets. The wooden chopping bowl with the double-bladed knife we wielded so briskly to cut up fruits, nuts, raisins, and the like for mince meat or fruit cakes can't be beaten by today's substitutes. Those marvelous old soup tureens doubled as cookie jars to hold mouth-watering molasses cookies brought up from the stone crock in the cellar.

Then there were the salt boxes, in which we stored the salt we bought in bulk, and the match boxes that hung over the stove. There were newspaper racks that also had places for brushes and combs. In our house, the rack hung over the sink. Elsewhere on the walls were special calendars, souvenir plates. Every family member had his or her own napkin ring — usually made of silver with initials or names engraved, and silver mugs and spoons were a favorite baby gift. I have one engraved "Grace for Grace," given me by my Aunt Grace Riddick, and Stanley had one with his name engraved on it, which he passed on to his namesake.

In many houses the butter churn made a good umbrella stand when churning was out; and butter paddles and molds are much sought after today. We used wooden knife and fork holders that we carried to the table. Every cook had her favorite wooden spoon, three-tined fork, butcher knife, rolling pin, iron griddle, and the special big coffee cup that she used for measuring.

Most recipes, or "receipts," of those days seem as crude to us today as many of the utensils they employed. Cooks depended on a "pinch" of this and a "handful" of that, or were instructed to add so many "gullups" of molasses (gullup, of course, was the sound the molasses made as it came from the jug). Many foods were to be baked in an "afternoon oven." Is it any wonder that instinct played so large a role in successful cooking?

I recall the fragrance of the spices and the lovely grain of the nutmeg after it had been grated. Today the spice cabinet, with its little drawers where the bags of cinnamon, sage, and ginger were stored, makes a wonderful holder for buttons, shells, or just plain odds and ends.

Despite the absence of labor-savers, there seemed to be time enough to do all sorts of fancy hand work — samplers, needlepoint chair seats, pillows, the hardanger, the cut-work, cross stitching, knitted lace and crocheted hug-me-tights — these are all treasured keepsakes today, though we took them for granted then.

Old advertising cards, bulletins, booklets, and premiums are always interesting. A Gold Medal flour booklet published in 1907 has rhymed instructions for home-made bread. An 1893 World's Fair bulletin shows the original "Bubbles" with Pears' Soap. Allen and Giners cigarettes came with one of a series of Birds of America cards included in each pack.

Advertising cards, illustrated with colored bouquets told us about "Dr. Dennis' System Renovator and Blood Purifying Syrum" or "Brown's Iron Bitters." The Athlophorus Co's Daisy touted their cure for rheumatism and neuralgia. And Dr. Peter Farhny's Alpenkrauter tonic was a mystical medicine that promised to make you feel better by the spoonful.

Calling cards with one's picture and name in fancy script, or little personalized gift-cards — some of them with miniature birds in real feathers — are choice remembrances.

Who wouldn't be pleased today to find one of those stone crock bottles that held ginger-beer and pop. Old crockery tea pots, coffee pots, and chocolate pots are really valuable now. Along with calendar plates, china mugs, and moustache cups, they were kept mostly for display in the dining room china cupboard.

Many of the hand-made utensils have been used for years and passed down in the family. Perhaps it is a lefse rolling pin or a pudding-stirrer (some call them Norwegian mix-masters) — a branch peeled of its bark, with several shortened branch ends trained up like prongs when the green wood was supple. When this was rotated between the palms, it kept the ingredients from sticking to the pan and really made a cream pudding without lumps. They tell me that lumberjacks used to make a similar gadget on which to dry their socks overnight. You could see them, looking like potato mashers, hanging from the rafters in the camps. Real potato mashers were carved out of wood, and they did smash a light potato!

Coverlets, patch-work quilts, rag rugs, hooked rugs, antimacassars, doilies, woven spreads, and table covers are passed from generation to generation, too. Clothing wore out, though it did last longer than many things do today. The big problem was the washing and ironing of heavy materials, which was done with home made soap, a washboard, a copper water boiler. The clothes were wrung by hand or tortured through a hand wringer, and women got lots of exercise running back and forth to the stove, trying to keep the sad irons hot. Nowadays we see washboards used as bulletin boards and sad-irons, painted in Pennsylvania Dutch style, to serve as bookends or door stops.

Remember the old boot-jacks that helped Grandpa pull off his heavy boots? Remember buttonhooks, iron banks and nutcrackers, paperweights given as premiums? Remember the long paper beads we wound on knitting needles and varnished, then hung in the doorway for portieres? Remember the diaries, the tobacco cans, the pincushions? How practical then; how collectible now.

What's Wrong With Flag Waving?

For many years I've been a flag-waver, and for a good many of those years I've noticed the sophisticated cynicism with which most Americans note any expression of patriotism. That doesn't bother me. I'll go right on, expressing my love for my country and its flag, and just feeling darn glad that I am an American.

Maybe I feel the way I do because we weren't always Americans, although I do have one ancestor who fought in the Revolution. (I'm eligible for membership in the D.A.R. — in fact, I have received an invitation to become a member. But like Eleanor Roosevelt, I feel no kinship with a group who were so prejudiced as to refuse Marian Anderson the right to sing in their hall.) Other ancestors came at later dates from Scotland, Ireland, England, and Canada, and all of my husband's ancestors came in the 1850's, from Norway. And several returned to their native land to recruit new citizens for this new free land — America. How can we help being proud of them?

My earliest recollection of being proud of my heritage as an American goes back to a day in February of 1912, when Miss Colignon, our first grade teacher announced, "Children, this is important. We now have 48 stars in our country's flag. Two new states have been admitted to the Union." Miss Colignon was a tall, slender woman who wore the usual dress of a teacher of those days — a long black wool skirt and a white shirt-waist, with a white half-apron, to protect her skirt from the chalk dust. She reached up and pulled down a map of the United States from its case at the top of the blackboard. "Here are the new states, two new stars in our flag. New Mexico, which joined us in January, and now, on February 12th, Arizona. Here is Wisconsin, and we became a state in 1848. Thirteen stripes in our flag represent the 13 original colonies. Now there will be 48 white stars on the field of blue. The flag of our country. Long may she wave! Now, let's all stand and sing 'My Country 'Tis of Thee," Our voices rang out loud and clear, and my heart throbbed: "I am an American!"

Many times after that, my pride in being an American came to the fore. In those days, when flag waving wasn't belittled, we were consciously taught patriotism. We were reminded that men had died for the flag of our country. The red said, "Be Brave," the white, "Be Pure," and the blue, "Be True." Our readers recounted stories of our country's heroes. Our music teacher taught us songs of America, and our art teacher focused on native artists, while also studying the old masters. History books recalled famous Americans, and our geographies illustrated a divided America that was yet one. Proudly, we repeated the pledge of allegiance each day. The vastness of the land was only exceeded by the vastness of our love for, and pride in, America.

World War I came in my teen years. I remember how I sobbed when I learned that my father had joined the National Guard. And although he wouldn't have to go "over there," he did go to Camp McCoy for home-guard training. Even in fear, however, my pride won out.

Directly across the street from us lived "Grandpa" Grandy, a veteran of the Civil War. We spent many hours on his porch, listening to stories of his days in the Union Army cavalry. Our father often told us of Teddy Roosevelt's charge up San Juan Hill, so we felt we knew many of our country's heroes first-hand. When the Armistice came we were fired anew with pride in the Grand Old Flag.

The first glimpse I had of our state capitol also stirred my patriotism. Stanley and I were driving from Milwaukee to Madison; the time was about dusk, and as we came over the top of a hill, the golden dome of the Capitol met our eyes. I knew that the building was fashioned after the one in Washington, which I was not to see until some years later. In that magical moment in Madison, my mind and heart said, "How wonderful to be an American!"

My patriotism derives from many sources—the ancestors who chose to come to this country rather than live anywhere else in the world, the ones who fought in the Revolution, and the others who defended the Union in the Civil War. But the strongest strain of my feeling for my country arises from my recognition of our freedoms. I have the freedom to live where I want, to worship as I want, to speak as I desire. I have freedom from want—even the freedom to cook as I please, be it ethnic dishes or good old midwest American favorites! I can vote as I choose. I can rise as high as my abilities can carry me, perhaps even to the highest office in the land.

Many moments stand out in my memory as times when I was proud to be an American. Checking in the cherry pails of German war prisoners, who were awed by the vastness of our land. My first glimpse of the Florida Everglades, and the view from the torch of the Statue of Liberty. The grandeur of the Grand Canyon at sunset, when two deer poised near the edge, close beside me. The blue of the Pacific. The sacred feeling of a Presence in the chapel of the United Nations. The Fourth of July parade, when the youngsters decorated their bikes and wagons with bunting. The patchwork countryside viewed from an airplane. Mark Twain's Hannibal, Mo., the Lincoln Memorial, Washington's monument and Mount Vernon. Commencement exercises signifying the equal opportunity available to all. The many wonders of this country that I have not seen, but can study from books or T.V. All of these spell AMERICA to me, and in these, today and everyday, I am proud of being an AMERICAN.

No More Party Line

The news item read: "The party line telephone in Wisconsin will soon be relegated to history. That is the forecast of the Public Service Commission."

No party line? I can't believe it! What memories that brings back of those old-time long-geared phone boxes with the crank on the side so you could ring *one* for central, or two short and one long, one long and three short for neighbors in an emergency, or just to "voss" as Grandma used to say. Back in my youth, when I visited on the farm in summertime, I was fascinated with their telephone. We didn't have one at home yet. Crank! — R-r-r-ing! "Operator, will you get me Doc Schuyler? My cow's got the bloat," or "Operator, ring the feed store at the Bay for me, please." Click, click, click: you could hear all the receivers going up all along the line — this was the grapevine, part of the daily news. Besides, if someone had an emergency all of the neighbors knew, and could give a helping hand.

In my early teens I remember we had our phone installed at home. Ours was a four party line, but our box had no crank; central answered when we took up the receiver, and we gave her the number we wanted to call. Sometimes there'd be someone talking when we lifted the receiver. But our folks were very insistent that we hang up then — no listening in. When sibling interference riled me up when my friend Genevieve and I were making plans, I'd hang up and run the two and a half blocks over to her house and deliver my message personally. Later, during the war years, Papa had a private line installed; the bank thought it expedient, in case of a business emergency. Then we had a telephone on a stand — we could sit down and talk.

Not until we opened the restaurant did I come in contact with the long phone-box party line again. We were nearly a mile out of town and the phones there were owned by a small company with thirteen subscribers, all on the same line with no business phone available. Especially for someone new to the business, it was difficult to listen and sort out those myriad rings, to be sure the one we answered *was* two-long-and-one-short. Our kitchen then hadn't been enlarged, so the phone was in fairly easy reach, but at serving time the one nearest stopped what she was doing and jotted down the take-out order, the reservations, or answered questions about meal prices. Sometimes the party at the other end had really wanted two-shorts-and-a-long, and "What the heck are *you* doing on the line, anyway?"

Of one thing I could be really sure: just let me get my hands in the roll dough and our ring came through loud and clear. Even the wax paper I kept handy to protect the receiver and my hands didn't keep the pen and notepad from getting covered.

I remember the little aggravations which were multiplied by the number of patrons on the line. The slight buzz on the line gave warning that Nosie Rosie was listening. Sometimes it was Rhoda Rumor, who spread news faster than any reports on T.V., or Babbling Bertha, who never gave up the line as long as she had breath to chatter on. Never mind if you had to get word downtown for Father-dear to bring home extra fish or hamburger—her gossip was more important. We had one practical joker who thought it hilarious to ring us at two a.m. and order ten boxes of chicken. (Maybe he felt he was paying us back because he heard our ring so late on prom or Sadie Hawkins' night, when worried parents called to see if their young ones had left for home yet.) We did excuse Hard-of-Hearing Harry, who interrupted most every incoming call, making sure it wasn't his ring.

Our neighbor told of talking with her sister from downtown one day, when she heard the sound of someone practicing on the piano. "Who's that?" her sister asked. "Oh, you might know, it's Mrs. Holmson; she's always rubbering." And, before a receiver banged, they heard: "Well, it ain't either me!"

There were redeeming features. We truly appreciated the neighbor who'd phone to say he was sending some customers over, and the friendly farmer who called to give us weather information daily. If we answered a ring by mistake we were happy when they graciously accepted our apology. There were folks who served as employment agencies, referring would-be workers to us, and real estate agents, on the lookout for good buys for retirees. If we could have hung on the line, we might have picked up some good recipes or household hints. There were watch-dogs, too, those loyal folks who would call the police in a hurry if they'd spied unusual goings-on about the place at night.

Man does not live by telephone alone, but that trusty box on the wall was second in importance only to our stoves and refrigerators. We begged for an extra phone upstairs, or at least a bell on the stairway since we couldn't hear the faint buzz from the kitchen up in our living quarters. But, no, so we made calls to the family in early morning, and instructed them to call before closing time. So, we usually had an audience to hear our affairs broadcast.

The party line regulated our political, spiritual, and social lives. There were always at hand those with educational, legal, or financial advice. A proper quorum was even available for a conference, if we wanted one. The party line gave us confidence that we'd be notified of up-coming weddings, birthdays or anniversaries, reports of meetings we were too busy to attend, or even the call to pick up Bob after the matinee, or Mary from play rehearsal. By process of elimination we learned, too, the best person from whom to buy fresh vegetables or fruits, scandal hot off the griddle, first aid for ailing appliances. Dear friends and gentle people — for many their lives revolved around that ring of the phone.

Then, after a couple of years, the lone subscriber with a private line moved away, and we inherited privacy. Our gratitude to party line should include the call we received at 1:15 a.m. a cold night in December. We had over a hundred after-the-winter-prom reservations confirmed, when at eight-thirty in the morning I called the doctor to come for what looked like a heart attack for Stanley. Another call brought the ambulance and all that day I commuted between the hospital and back to the restaurant to prepare what I could for the evening — no way of cancelling out those kids. An accommodating salesman detoured into Green Bay to alert Ruth, who had just moved, and whose phone was not yet installed. Our loyal help were there to serve, and at eleven a girlhood friend walked in and said, "Tell me what to do." Cars zipped up the hill; young folks filled the dining room, dressed in lovely pastel prom dresses and formal dress. Chicken in a basket, shrimp, perch plates, hamburgers, and Stanley's famous "ziggies" went through the swinging door as fast as we could manage. We had only one table left to serve when the phone's jangle sent me running. "Grace," Dr. Beck's voice came over the line to me, "I just wanted you to know that Stanley's out of danger." I choked out a "Thank God!" but someone else served that last table—I was limp as a dish rag.

Many calls ring a memory. The telegram from San Diego, phoned in saying Gil's ship was in, and would Ruth and the baby come out to be with him. Then the call from the florist an hour after she'd left, asking if he should deliver her anniversary flowers which had been on order. The message telling us Mary would be a bride. The call from Alameda that Bob had reached boot camp. Grandchildren on the way, deaths, weddings, baptisms. Calls on Mother's Day, in the midst of serving an overflowing room of mothers. Thanksgiving, Christmas, birthday calls. Calls from lonely offspring—just so good to hear your voice. What would we have done without party line communication?

You were capricious, Party Line, but then so are we all. You served us well, despite your limitations. It wasn't your fault that our business didn't permit us to join the preferred company of friendly souls willing and eager to pass along information, recipes, or censorship of movie programs. When the subscription company sold out to Wisconsin Telephone Company and we once more were part of a city phone system, when we actually got an extension phone upstairs and no longer had to turn the crank to ring for the operator, there was a bit of regret for all the memories you had given us. Now, as retirees, your long box hangs on our dining room wall—no batteries inside, but still an important piece of memorabilia we treasure, along with those memories of more active days. We will mourn your passing, Party Line. You deserve a ringing tribute (perhaps two longs and a short?) for the decades you went beyond the call of duty to serve us through long waits, noisy listeners, futile attempts to reach central to put through that all important call. You served us well, Party Line! Thank You! Hail and farewell!

Christmas 1931

Dusk was coming on. The car moved slowly in the whirling snow. The wind whipped the falling flakes, whirling them at the car and lashing the bare branches of trees along the roadside. We were on our way to Madison with Cliff and Clara Herlache. They were looking forward to Christmas with her folks, while Stanley and I had a different errand. "Does that blowing snow make it hard driving?" I asked. "No, just hampers visibility once in awhile. Worried?" "Not really," I said, but my thoughts were on a possible blizzard, and the little ready money we had wouldn't go far in helping being towed out, nor pay for storm-bound lodging and food.

As we rode on, I peered through the window at the isolated farm houses along the way. Everything was still. Here and there a lighted Christmas tree gleamed. Several homes had Christmas wreaths on the door. Then I saw it.

"Look," I cried, "there's one—the candle in the window, to light the Christ Child on His way! Now it's beginning to look like Christmas." I had begun to think that no one believed in Christmas traditions anymore.

The folks at home must be concerned, wondering if the snow would intensify. It seemed a shame to desert our baby on her first Christmas, but Grandma and Grandpa would take good care of her, and she was too young, anyway, to realize it was Christmas. She'd be happy with the stuffed doll I'd made, and the soft rubber ball. Still, I missed her. Too bad we couldn't have brought her along. I brushed a bit of lint off my coat, noticing how worn the edge and the buttonholes were getting. But coats didn't matter. If only . . .

Would Keith see a lighted candle flickering in the window, would he hear Christmas Carols on the radio, and would anyone read "The Night Before Christmas" to him? I sighed and resigned myself to counting outdoor decorations.

On and on we went; then, as we came to the brow of a hill the lighted dome of the Capitol loomed ahead. "Look, Stanley!" I said, "that's our Christmas tree this year! Isn't it beautiful?"

It was strange to wake up Christmas morning in a hotel room. It took a few moments to adjust to the change, to remember why we were here. I turned the knobs of the little table radio, and sounds of Christmas carols filled the air. I reached over to wake Stanley and say, "Merry Christmas!"

It still seemed unreal as we ate breakfast in the hotel dining room. There were festive touches on each table, and a large tree with glowing lights, colored glass baubles, and dripping icicles near the door. But few guests were about. Most folks had gone home for the holidays. I tried to keep up sprightly conversation, but I knew that Stanley was as anxious as I to get going.

At exactly ten o'clock we stood at the door of the Orthopedic Hospital, our arms filled with small packages. The door was locked. A nurse peeped out, and said, "Visiting hours aren't till two. Sorry, I can't let you in now. We're just bringing the children back from the party."

"We know. We planned to come back again this afternoon. But couldn't we just see him for a little while this morning?" I was near tears.

An intern walked into the room, and the nurse conferred with him briefly. Then she turned to us, smiling. "It's all right. You can see him. You've come so far, and after all, it's Christmas."

The everyday face of the hospital had changed. Sprays of evergreen and red and green bells hung in the halls, and the nurse told us that the Girl Scouts had decorated for the party. One whole wall had been rolled aside, revealing a huge auditorium. There a ceiling-high tree sparkled with lights and multi-colored glass balls. Strains of "Jingle Bells" filled the air. There was hubbub in the room, too. Nurses and interns were pushing hospital beds and children in wheelchairs back to their respective wards. Laughing, squealing children were displaying gifts and candy treats. Little hands clutched soft toys and candy canes.

Such a spirit of joy prevailed that one forgot to notice the handicaps of the little ones. There was even a Santa, "ho, ho, ho-ing" as he waved goodby to the youngsters. Oh, here it was really Christmas!

We hurried down the corridor, peering into the traveling cribs for Keith's precious face. But he was already back in his room with his eleven roommates. The curly blond head bobbed up and down, despite the restraint of the traction chin-strap. Blue eyes danced, and his happy smile grew wider as he called out, "Mommy—Daddy—see what I got!"

We walked over to his crib. With feet in stirrups and head in traction it seemed so torturous. Yet the doctors had assured us that this relieved the pressure on the insidious thing happening to his vertebrae; he was really far more comfortable this way.

He held up a pink popcorn ball, and for just a moment I panicked. Should he have that? Could he choke on it? I'd always been so careful; he'd never had any before. Then, with an effort, I relaxed. He'd manage. And after all, it was Christmas.

We hugged him as best we could and looked at the array of toys and gifts on his bed. Small things we had made and sent ahead in case the weather had prevented this trip. On other children's beds we recognized more homemade gifts, and the nurse told us that the Girl Scouts and Salvation Army had provided things for the children who would have been forgotten. The Wise Men had brought gifts of gold and frankincense and myrrh. Strangers had brought love. How grateful we were! We moved about the ward, distributing the inexpensive presents we had brought for Keith and the other children. Nurses came in, dispensing medicine, adjusting weights, and easing cast-enclosed legs or arms where possible, making them more comfortable. We saw no fear in the youngsters' faces as the interns and nurses ministered to them, only friendly smiles.

After a little the aides came in with the dinner trays. On each one a fat marshmallow Santa added to the holiday spirit. Chicken, vegetables, dishes of Jello, and, at the sight of ice cream, squeals of delight.

"We have to go now, Keith, and get our dinner," Stanley told the boy as the nurse prepared to feed him. "But we'll be back this afternoon. See you then." Keith waved happily, then opened his mouth for the spoonful of food. The traction harness didn't permit his sitting up to feed himself.

It was quiet now in the corridor. The auditorium wall had been rolled back in place. Hospital business went on as usual with calm efficiency.

As we reentered the lobby, I reached for Stanley's hand. He squeezed mine understandingly. We both knew that Keith wouldn't see another Christmas.

Don't Let Your Guard Down

"You asked those gypsies in for a cup of tea?" The policeman's voice was incredulous. He no doubt thought I was some kind of kook. My friend had called him when I told her I'd had a gypsy visit.

Stanley's brother James had taken us to the clinic that morning. There was an almost two hour wait before Stanley saw the doctor, but James sat patiently in the lobby waiting for us. We got home about twelve forty-five, and sat and visited awhile. James said he didn't want any lunch. When he left, I went out into the kitchen to put the teakettle on and make some sandwiches. I was slicing the cold roast beef when I hear Stanley call: "GRACE! There's someone here to see you."

As soon as I got back to the living room a queer feeling down the length of my spine told me something was wrong. Women don't just walk into a stranger's house without a purpose. (I know who you are, I thought, looking closely at the two.)

"Hello! We came see you; we get lonesome." They stood beside Stanley's chair, boldly smiling. Both had dark hair, dark eyes, olive skin. They were, perhaps, in their late twenties. One had an odd, flattened-out nose. She looked dowdy and careless, though her rose-colored blouse and the full skirt which reached to mid calf were clean but wrinkled. The other, younger and better looking, had curled and fluffy hair cut to almost shoulder length. Her full skirt was just below the knee; she wore a striped knit top. Black eyes darted here and there, cataloging the room's contents.

(Oh my gosh! I forgot to lock the door when James left. I KNEW these people were around. How could I let my guard down like that! These are the ones who get into women's homes while they were in the garden or hanging clothes, stealing things and even trying to choke one poor women. They must have thought I was alone, too. But I can't let them know that Stanley needs help to get around.) "Where do you live?" "Down the street."

"In that red brick house in the next block?" They nodded, "That's the one." (Aha, I know how to trap you. Those are Coast Guard people who live there.)

"We're just going to have lunch. Won't you have a cup of tea?" (I'm not going to give them a chance to be in a room we're not in.)

"Fluffy" followed me into the kitchen; "Flat-nose" stopped in the dining room. Both women rushed to the window, "What a beautiful view!" That didn't fool me. I knew they were looking for a back exit. But ours was another story above the bay; no way to get off the back porch.

Fluffy was behind me as I opened the refrigerator door to take out the butter. I could feel her tabulating the contents. She edged over closer to the door of Stanley's room, peering in to check his files and the table that served as his desk, meanwhile checking the silver drawer as I opened that to set the table. I took the lid off the teapot, and she lifted the kettle and filled the teapot without so much as a by your leave. "Too much," I said and put in another tea bag. She was not taking over in my house. I carried in the teapot, sandwiches, and napkins, told them to come to the table, and went in to help Stanley to the table and set his walker behind his chair.

Flat-nose moved away from the china cabinet; she was ogling Grandma's china and crystal. "Knock it off!" I thought.

I offered them only tea; we ate the sandwiches. Before we started to eat I said the grace we had always used. Flat-nose said, "You Catholic?" "No, are you?" "Yes." "Where do you go: Corpus Christi?" "Yes," they both nodded, and I thought, "Keep it up. You're tricking yourself," and added, "I know lots of people who go up there."

Fluffy looked at the table and said, "Sugar?" and Flat-nose pointed to the china cabinet. Down on the third shelf, behind the vinegar cruets was the Fostoria bowl with lump sugar. Nothing wrong with her eyesight. I set the sugar on the table, poured the tea, and gave Stanley his medicine.

"Where do you come from?" I inquired. "Michigan." "What town?" "Villa." "In Upper Michigan?" She nodded. (I'll bet.)

Stanley began to tell them about Upper Michigan and that he had relatives there. I was afraid he might mention the restaurant. No way did I want them to know that. But Fluffy simpered, "How old he?" and I said "He's the same age I am."

"He look old; you not old. You so good to him." Don't try buttering me up! They both kept calling me Momma, and that made me mad, too.

"He has been sick. Before that he was a big handsome man." (Oh, I shouldn't have said that — if they think he's weak they might try overpowering him like they did those two women out in the country.)

Stanley said, "Grace, get that picture of the four of us boys on my dresser." I gave him a warning look and passed it off with, "Not now, Stanley." I wasn't having Fluffy get anywhere near his room.

"You have such beautiful things." I was expecting some comment, and told her our things were only beautiful to us, because they had belonged to our families, and would go to our children.

"You own such a big house." (Fishing, are you? I let her know we rented; didn't even have a car.)

"How much rent you pay?" "We pay what we have to." "Too much," she murmured. The *Door County Advocate* lay on the buffet. Stanley pointed to it, and ever the proud husband, said, "Grace wrote that. See, her picture's in there."

"You write that? Read it to us."

"No, you can read it yourself." (I could feel the vibes; they were getting a little wary of me. And Stanley was on to them, too.)

Broad nose, her dangling gold earrings bouncing, tried again, "Who live upstairs?" That was my chance — "Two men, father and son. They work over at the shipyard, should be coming home soon. And they have a BIG DOG, very friendly if you know him, but look out if you don't!" I could see their nervousness now. Why hadn't I thought of Rocky before? Fluffy asked for a glass of water so she could "take her medicine." That was a ruse I'd heard of before. One would ask for a glass of water; the other would hunt for money or something else she could steal. I brought it to the table, and gave her a level look as she took out aspirin. Now I was getting a bit antsy. They knew Stanley needed help. If they both tried pushing him over he'd be helpless once down on the floor. But, I told myself, he'd get in some pretty good licks first; his arms were strong from having to push himself up from his chair. I knew, too, that I would be no match for the two.

But they had decided it was time to leave. Two men coming home and a big dog to contend with was too much. I walked with them to the door, saw them go down past the mailboxes on the corner and then disappear. Someone must have been waiting to pick them up. As I walked back through the room (after locking the screen door!) I noticed my purse sitting on the sofa, where I'd set it down when we got home. We were eating strawberries when Frances called and I told her about the visitors. "I'll call the police, maybe they can catch them." The police were courteous, but they found no trace. My friend in the country told me how those same women had mauled her and tried to choke her, because she wouldn't give them money, and even pulled the phone off the wall. The news was on the scanner, but no results. They worked the other end of town a few days later. I should have asked them to read my fortune in tea leaves! But I keep the door locked now.

A New Grave

It was mid-afternoon; the orchard was hot and the sounds seemed to press
down—the singing, quarreling, laughing voices, most in Spanish, as
the pickers neared the end of the day's work. Suddenly a young Mexican
boy came running up to the shed, where I was punching pickers' tickets,
crying: "Señora! Over there! Over in that little cemetery! There's a new
grave!" As he spoke, a ring of curious Mexicans moved in toward the shed.

I questioned him carefully, but his story was the same. It wasn't near
the road; it was over closer to the tall pines, a new grave, and a little one.

Looking about nervously, I spied Ed, the hired man, coming down the
row, hauling a load of empty crates behind the tractor. Soon he would
bring the truck in, to be loaded with the cherries picked today. The trucks
waited in line at the Fruit Growers till the fruit was dumped in the big
tanks of water and sent, down an assembly line, for processing.

Quickly, I explained what the youngster had told me. Ed disclaimed
any knowledge of the grave, so, after punching his ticket and telling him
to keep an eye on the card rack, I followed Pablo to the old family burying
plot. Recently, there had been a stabbing in another orchard, so this news
made me a little edgy. I knew we would be followed.

The cemetery was in one corner of the once eighty-acre farm that was
the old homestead. Twenty years ago about half had been planted to cherry
orchard. It really was a lovely spot—tall pine trees hid it from the road,
and a grove of elm and maple divided it from the orchard on the other
side. The family plot was surrounded by a white picket fence, rather dilapi-
dated now, and huge lilac bushes grew inside. Here, I knew, were the graves
of Great-grandma's sister, who had lived with them for a time, and the
smaller grave of four year old Delia, who had died of diphtheria. Near
the biggest elm was the grave of Job Sweet, a Civil war veteran, who had
worked on the farm. (Every year the children and I placed a small flag,
and a bouquet of wild flowers on the grave.) Nearby was the grave of an-

other hired man, who, they had told us, had lost his way home in a blizzard, and was found frozen to death next morning. Later, the cemetery was acquired by the township, and about twenty or more bodies were buried there. Of late years it had been used as a potter's field, so it was puzzling to hear of a new occupant.

As I followed Pablo, my heart began beating faster, and I wondered just what I would find. Yes—there was a new grave, the mound of dirt heaped high and smoothed over. And it was a little one. Had a child been killed and buried? What should I do? How could I find out?

I started back to the orchard. Then I saw Stanley's car, as he came back from town to help load the full containers of cherries for their trip to the Fruit Growers. I motioned for him to stop, and explained what Pablo had discovered. He got out of the car and went over to see for himself. When he returned, he told me he was going over to see the sheriff to try to unravel the mystery. I returned to my place as checker. All around me I could hear buzzing, and knew the pickers were speculating and wondering, too.

The next hour seemed to drag. When the pickers carried in pails to check they did so warily, then went quickly back to their trees. At last Stanley returned. We all crowded around the car, anxious to hear what he had found out. He had talked with the sheriff first; then they had gone to see the undertaker. They were told that an Indian family, here in the county for cherry picking, had lost a small baby. The city had authorized burying it in the little cemetery. There had been no funeral.

Soberly we went back to the cherries, the mystery cleared up; but that evening a bouquet of black-eyed-susans graced the little grave.

GOOD ENOUGH
FOR THE HELP

A Lonesome Fireplace
Looking For A Home

For fourteen years the fieldstone fireplace stood, like a sentinel, waiting for a home. It had been a part of a log home that had burned to the ground one evening in September 1935. The owners were our neighbors. We lived just across the orchard from them, on the old Svend Samuelson homestead. We had watched that house being built two years ago, and we saw its demise.

Our two girls, Ruth, four, and Mary, one, had been in bed for a good half hour when we heard Ruth call: "Daddy! We want some popcorn, too." "Why, I'm not popping corn. Go to sleep now," Stanley said.

"Oh yes you are. We can hear it popping."

We hurried to the girls' room. The bright glow coming through the windows was startling. And there *was* a popping sound, like firecrackers on a string. Over the granary roof and through the cherry trees we could see flames shooting up and black smoke roiling.

"Backey's house is on fire!" Stanley yelled, and he was off, moving swiftly for such a big man. "Call the fire department!" he called back over his shoulder. We saw his frame silhouetted against the blaze. The girls were crying; I ran in a daze to the kitchen telephone and rang for the operator. They already knew about the fire; the operator told me the fire engine was at the scene. I shook as I got Mary into her clothes. Carrying her, and holding Ruth by the hand, I made my way through the orchard to Backey's.

The house looked like a huge furnace, flames and smoke billowing out, shooting higher and higher. The sky over the bay glowed red; it was bright as daylight. Firemen were struggling to turn the force of the water on the fire, but we could see it was too late to save the house. Neighbor men were milling about, trying to save whatever furniture and belongings they could, but not much could be salvaged. The heat was intense. Sparks flew; the noise of popping shingles was frightening. We asked if everyone got out safely and were told they had.

Gladys Backey stood at one side, desolately holding the hands of her two little girls. Someone told us that she, five months pregnant, had managed to get the girls and her cedar chest out through the window. As I moved to try to comfort her, it seemed we were all acting as in a dream, dazed, and yet those flames held a fascination for us all. Our girls were weeping as they saw their little friends homeless. The hopelessness of the situation appalled me.

The logs burned fiercely. We heard someone say that faulty wiring had caused the fire. No one could get near the building now; all furnishings, everything was lost. We stood watching numbly as their few belongings were loaded on a truck, to be taken to Ken's folks' home till plans could be made. The family would stay there. What a formidable prospect: Depression years, out of work, savings all used, and now their home gone.

We walked back home through the orchard, dejectedly, feeling grief for their loss, and because we could be of so little help. Yet we were grateful there had been no loss of life. There was no hope of rebuilding after the debris was cleared; and the fireplace, the only thing left intact, stood amid the ruins, starkly showing through the grove of white birch, like a monument.

In 1949 we moved back to Door County. Stanley's work as a State Produce Inspector had taken us to the southeastern part of the state, and we lived in Greendale. Five of us now; our Bob was born in 1940. From Greendale we went to Marshalltown, Iowa. Stanley was sales manager for a mineral feed firm. But home was Door County, and we came back. We bought the land at the other side of the old homestead, where that lonesome fireplace stood, cleared the land of second growth, and built a restaurant on the spot, incorporating that lone sentinel into the large concrete block building. Our living quarters were on the second floor. The only repair needed on the fireplace was to replace two large stones just below and to the right of the new mantel. The fireplace had found a home.

A Motto. The Help.

I had never had the faintest desire to run a restaurant. I didn't know any-thing about it, and, except for a summer's work at Brookside Tea Gardens in the early twenties, I'd never been in a restaurant kitchen. I loved our rooms upstairs, and had a great time decorating them. The location was lovely, too, with the view of surrounding orchards, the bay and the little grove by the road that ran down to the creek, where giant trees overhung the water and where I daily had a rendezvous with beauty.

But Stanley had his mind made up. He was sure a restaurant in that location would be a success. He did most of the construction himself, with the help of two vagrants who stayed after the cherry season was over. My father died in September, and we moved into mother's house for the win-ter. Ruth went to Door Kewaunee Normal; Mary was a sophomore in high school and Bob a fourth grader, lucky enough to get into Selma Whit-ford's class. We moved into our new home and business place early in May. The restaurant was to open about May 28.

I was sewing the bird print curtains for my little upstairs kitchen when I heard the announcer on the "Grand Slam" game program on radio say: "Mrs. Grace Samuelson, from Sturgeon Bay, Wisconsin, has won three prizes today: a Samsonite luggage set, a floor polisher, and a wrist watch." (All that for suggesting three songs to be played so the contestant could guess the titles.) I was so excited that I rushed down into the yard, where the men were clearing out a parking lot and attempting to move a large birch clump. The men were all properly impressed with my good luck. Just as I was about to go upstairs again a woman drove up, a reporter from the *Door County Advocate*. She wanted to interview the owners of the new restaurant, and we invited her up to our living quarters. I remained quiet throughout most of her questioning, after Stanley had given her a tour of the building. Then, the bomb fell.

"This should be a very popular place; such a beautiful location, attractive atmosphere, and with reasonable prices people will surely be anxious to come. Who is going to do your cooking?"

I opened my mouth to tell her we hadn't yet hired a chef, but Stanley answered, "Well, my wife's always been a good cook. I'm sure she can manage just fine." I was speechless. Never in my wildest dreams had I thought of cooking in a restaurant. I'd never even been chairman at church suppers. The walls rang with my protests when the reporter left. It did me no good. Stanley was sure that I could do it. The kids thought it would be fun. "You can do it; we'll help you."

So we launched a new project, learning the ropes as we went along: into a uniform and out into a spanking new kitchen to discover how to please the public; discovering that our "help" were truly loyal friends; hunting for quantity recipes, for quick and easy — and reliable — ways of food preparation; family life relegated to odd "free" hours; no chance for movies or other entertainment; adjusting menus and eliminating things that took too long to prepare, or were hard to get. We had help from an unexpected source. The salesmen, realizing how green I was at this, suggested ways to speed up serving, and brought special recipes from other restaurants.

On May 23, 1950, the *Door County Advocate* announced that a new restaurant, SAMUELSON'S, would open on Sunday, May 28, and that we were equipped to handle wholesale smoked and fresh fish, and custom smoking. (Although our equipment and know-how were adequate for this phase of the business, we had to give up that plan; there was not enough fish available for the wholesale market, and a good thing, too, since we had enough to cope with in establishing a restaurant.)

Opening day arrived. We gave it our best, with the welcome help of family, friends, relatives, and our new employees. The people came. They ate the turkey with dressing or the ham with horse-radish sauce. We peeled and cooked kettle after kettle of potatoes to mash. We sent the plates out as fast as we could, and Stanley sliced the big Oriole hams and carved the turkeys. The home-made rolls and apple and cherry pies seemed to melt away. The coffee pots were emptied fast, and, as the last full and happy customers left, we almost collapsed from exhaustion. We were too tired to eat, although there was food left. We'd made it.

Gradually a pattern formed. We learned to cope with schedules, to take reservations for groups and parties in our stride, found that chicken in a box was a very good item. I learned the intricacies of the French fryer, how to read an order and pigeonhole the information. Stanley was promoted to the dining room, where he was maître d', keeping the coffee cups filled and handing out menus. The room with the "lonesome" fireplace became a much used private dining room. The thirteen-party telephone line kept ringing with reservations, orders for chicken to go, and inquiries about prices.

If I had thought I'd hear someone say, "What's a nice person like you doing working in a restaurant?" I was disappointed. People were very nice to me, but it was time I showed my mettle. I had to dig in and realize that I, too, was "help." Learning restaurant lingo was fun, though we really never talked very much restaurant language. One of our first big parties, a class reunion for a hundred, was an education for me. We knew we'd need extra help to get all that food ready, and the woman who came in to help us was experienced in some restaurants, though not in our ways. She and Alice and I kept busy all that Saturday morning, peeling apples and making eighteen apple pies. We had an apple peeler, which helped a lot, but there still was the coring and slicing. Our Mrs. New Help kept telling us she wanted a pie that was apple-full, and believe me, hers were heaped so high that when baked the crust stood up like a shell, and the apples weren't all cooked through. But she was a pleasant person, and when I asked her to cook the pork chops we were all having at noon she kept chirping, "Pork chops is my favorite vegetable." The picture I carry in my mind is of her sitting almost all day Sunday, peeling potatoes for fries and mashing, all the while talking a steady stream. Her husband used to come to collect her pay, and I got the idea she hadn't much to say about that.

When we lived in Greendale I had a column in that weekly paper, "Over The Back Fence." One week I had written, "Nothing is appreciated like appreciation," but when it came out in the paper it just said, "Nothing is appreciated." I was beginning to feel that way those first years in the restaurant, as the help, the family and I learned to adjust to one another, and I learned the vagaries of restaurant life. We went through all the learning steps. As time went on our menus changed dramatically from the ambitious forty-item list (everything from whale steak and frogs legs to turkey and beef). The major problem was getting the various orders to come out at the same time. It was as difficult for us as a new bride's adjustment. And, when we in the kitchen couldn't get the orders out fast enough, it was the girls in the dining room who took the ribbing: "Did they have to catch that chicken first?" "I can broil fish in fifteen minutes at home."

(Maybe so, but at home there weren't five or six orders that had to go on first.) We began to feel as if we were walking through waist deep water, taking one step forward and two back. We learned to anticipate the rush days and nights: "Put on your roller skates, girls."

Madman's Delight, or Moron's Delight: that's the name given to a dessert Don Reynolds invented, cherry pie ala mode with a generous covering of chocolate syrup. Stanley named a hamburger plate a Ziggy, to glorify the American hamburger as Ziegfield did the American girl. What a lot of misnomers for that we heard: Ziggyburgers, hot Ziggety, Zip a dee Burgers, spittleburgers, jiffyburgers, Zissy, Zigger — we filled them all. It was one of the favorite orders. In secret corners of the kitchen we nicknamed some predictable patrons: Brown chicken, Picky-ficky, or Rushie Gussie, always in a hurry when he came in but lingering to visit till late. The man who confided he had a "sensible" stomach. The patrons so immersed in conversation they didn't realize they were eating with the meat fork. The family with the scavenger boy. They ordered for all the rest of the family, but he had to scavenge what he could from their plates.

The Men's Club of our church furnished us prayer cards to put on the tables. These had table graces for Catholic, Protestant, and Jewish faiths. Many people used them, and we had some cottage people and others who joined hands and said grace, like the Waltons. We felt that was really homelike.

Adjusting to people's wants, to new menus, to bifocals that required orders down on the table on a spindle rather than up on a clipboard, I went through my apprenticeship, as did all our help. One year I was honored by having a pedigreed cow named for me, June informed me. I was put down when I overheard one girl say, "Bring those pots and pans over to Grace; she *likes* to wash dishes." Our spaghetti sauce made such a hit that we were hard put to keep enough on hand, and we joked about a Scots-Irish cook making Italian spaghetti with Swedish meat balls, and learned never to put the tiny cup of hot peppers on unless especially ordered. When I was fixing a take-out order one night, the man asked me, "I suppose that's *al dente*?" When I picked up a strand in my fingers to pinch it for doneness, he seemed a little taken back. There were some folks who thought that all a cook read was a recipe book. Still, I had some marvelous conversations with those folks who called for take out orders. Getting a reservation a half hour before serving time and asking for a birthday cake could stymie one, but it's been done.

The little old lady who gave us our kitchen motto was in the private dining room with a family group. She told Helen, "You can take those beans back. Didn't touch 'em." "Mother! They never do that!" "Well, it's good enough for the help." Once Lois carried hot rolls in and a lady asked for cherry coffee cake she'd heard about. "Oh, that's just for the help." Good enough!

Home Cooking? Heaven Forbid!

We were in Manitowoc to get a piece of restaurant equipment a week or so before our opening. Stanley said he was going to take me to a little cafe where you could get the best bean soup. I'd been hooked on bean soup ever since I was a child. We had baked beans every Saturday night of our lives, and, when Mama poured the cooked yellow-eyed beans into the big brown bean pot, she always left a cupful in the kettle for me. Bean soup was my specialty. I added rice, more water, a smidgin of onion, a chunk of butter, and it simmered an hour while I finished my Saturday chores. While Vera and Verna ate sandwiches on Saturday noons, I ate my soup, with more butter and broken crackers. (I don't know how it was I was allowed to break crackers in bean soup; we couldn't do that at the dinner table. We had to bite into those big soda crackers that came by the case.) The girls always called me the "Russian." I didn't care, and I still like bean soup.

We went into the small cafe where a big sign in the window proclaimed: HOME COOKING. The place was nice and clean. There were checkered cloths on the tables and a man and wife working. They weren't very busy that afternoon. I watched as the lady took a gallon jar of soup from the refrigerator, and spooned a cupful into a saucepan, then put a hot dog on the grill for Stanley. When the soup was served, I took one spoonful of soup and told Stanley, "I can't eat this. It's spoiled." The man was very solicitous. "Why, we just made that a week ago." I was horrified. I took a hot dog instead, but once outside the place I pointed to the sign and said, "NO home cooking in our restaurant!"

People were generous with their suggestions about that. "Why not?" they'd ask. "You serve home style cooking, bake all your own rolls and pies; you won't have a steam table. Why not capitalize on Home Cooking? You could advertise, Just Like Mother Used to Bake." Heavenly Days, I thought. Some mothers were rotten cooks. I should throw my lot in with them? My Scots-Irish stubbornness held fast. There never was a Home Cooking ad.

It was hard for a home made cook with home made helpers to avoid it, but we fixed meals in quantity, and the patrons came back for more. We'd get away from the standardized menu by making homey dishes for the help, and sometimes our kids would look in the refrigerator and say, "Isn't there ever anything good to eat in this place?" We all felt that way at times.

The experience of one of the help with Ma's cooking was unique. He told us that when he was sixteen years old he got his first job, washing dishes at a restaurant down town. He was surprised to know that hamburger could be something besides little hard balls like B-B shot. Pork chops at home were brittle chips. His Ma believed that everything should be cooked long and well, and the old wood range helped her do that. She was great at soups and stews. Her bread puddings and rice and raisin pudding were tasty, though you had to eat through a half inch of brown crust. Her knack with pies left something to be desired: NOBODY bakes pies like my Ma. . . . . . . Thank goodness! And I remembered the story about the bride who could never make pea soup like her mother-in-law's—until the day it got scorched when she was on the phone. "At last you've got the knack," he told her. "This tastes just like Ma's."

My own school of experience stemmed from pre-World War I days when everything started from scratch, and progressed through the Depression years when we learned to make do, finally graduating into family cooking. I thought it was great that I enjoyed working with yeast dough, since I had to bake two kinds of rolls every day that we were open, and, instead of one or two pies for dinner, I made ten or a dozen week nights and twenty to twenty-four Sundays. My cooking was surely not above reproach; there was just as much chance of failures in quantity cooking as home style. Crazy things happened, such as the day I was all ready to serve a Swiss steak dinner to a group of forty, decided that it needed a whiff more salt. The cover of the salt shaker fell off, and with it a small mountain of that white stuff. A quick scoop, and discarding the top portion saved the day, but I shook for an hour afterwards. I was rushing too fast one evening when I started to fix a chicken liver order, only to discover I'd grabbed the powdered sugar instead of the breading!

I almost cried the night two perfect halves of whitefish came off the broiler and one plopped off my oversize spatula onto the floor. I cheated a little. The order with the fallen fish had to wait while we deep fried another whitefish, then ran it under the broiler for the look of toasting. It looked good, and I hoped the customer didn't have to watch his cholesterol.

In the winter of 1962, we drove out to California, when Mary had her second baby, Chris. At that time one seldom saw fast food places except in the larger cities. Finding a good place to eat was a problem. We'd always been told that if you want good food stop where the truckers do. OK if you are looking for quantity, you'll surely get that. On the Oklahoma Panhandle we were stranded, along with at least twenty semi-truckers and as many travelers in cars, in a freak snowstorm. We managed to find a room in a small motel and then trudged through the drifts to find a place to eat. This one should be good, we thought: GRACE'S PLACE. The ark oiled floor was so slippery we almost fell in. You can't keep a place immaculate with so many tramping in the snow and slush. Greasy smoke filled the air, and a waitress in a food-spotted apron was buzzing around bringing heaping platefuls to the folks at the counter. Two truckers finished their coffee and made room for us. On the wall opposite a blackboard with ragged printing told us the special for the day was Polish sausage and sauerkraut. Our plates came, crammed with the sausage, sauerkraut, potato salad, boiled turnips, baked beans topped with two slices of buttered rye bread. I really did my best, but I couldn't manage very much of it. The waitress asked if everything was OK. I told her I was a little under the weather, but the husky cook at the stove glared at me, and, as Stanley paid the check I slunk out, knowing that I had committed the unpardonable sin: I'd turned up my nose at a plate of HOME COOKING.

Although we disdained the label of Home Cooking, we made an effort to keep the homey touch. We made birthday cakes for patrons, though never with elaborate decorating. Orders to fill for party sandwich loaves, for dips, canapes, hors d'oeuvres, specialties for birthdays or picnics — those were fun and provided variety for us. I'd never been to a cocktail party in my life, but the "fixin's" were fun to do. Weddings could have our personal touch, and anniversaries, and I really enjoyed the extra touches for group or club parties. We kept the homey touch in the private dining room, and I always thought I'd have time to sit and read there or listen to favorite radio programs. When we got television in 1954 that went upstairs. With both girls gone we had the front room for our living room once more. That was the winter Stanley had to spend three months in bed, since they thought his heart was acting up. One morning, when I was getting a tray ready for him, down in the restaurant kitchen, the florist drove up and handed me a beautiful azalea plant. "Oh, this must be for Stanley," I said. "No, it's for you; I'll stay till you read the card and then explain it to you." "But then it must be for Verna; she's in the hospital now." I read the card and was still more puzzled: "From your three Thursday morning sweethearts." "Whatever—?" It seems that the garbage men wanted to do something special for me and decided on that lovely plant, just because I asked them to come in Thursday mornings when they picked up the garbage. I truly enjoyed visiting with them, and they were undoubtedly the most complimentary customers, in return for pie and coffee. They wouldn't have had to make it up that long driveway; they could have told us to set the garbage cans out at the road. All this was before the Hefty plastic bags were on sale. We lined the kitchen cans with newspaper, and the last thing the boys did before leaving at night was to dump those cans into the larger ones outside. I recall a couple of times having to put on rubber gloves to sort through the potato peelings, eggshells, and bones and scraps to hunt for something lost, like a favorite paring knife, or the gear from the cabbage cutter. Sweet job!

Two homey touches we got quite by accident. I discovered a new relish the day we ran out of cranberries for the plates. Some cherry pie filling stood in the kettle; I added the juice from spiced apple pickles and a bit of allspice and cloves. We sent that out in the little souffle cups and received such enthusiasm we never again served cranberries. The invention was so much in demand that we started putting spiced cherries on each table in little glass dishes. We canned it and sold the thirty-three pints we got from each twenty-pound can of frozen cherries as fast as Betty could fill the jars. Because we had so many requests I had slips printed with individual recipes: four cups frozen cherries, thawed, 1 cup sugar and four level tablespoons cornstarch, cooked till thickened and transparent, then two tablespoons white vinegar added, and a teaspoon each powdered cloves and allspice. That was spiced cherry sauce.

The other touch was the violets in the window. I had convinced Stanley I'd just have one plant in each window, so that his inlaid covered sills wouldn't be damaged. Then I sneakily kept adding one or so more at a time. When the customers began to comment on the plants and ask about them, I let them think it was his idea. He really got to like them.

There was surely a personal touch in the place the night the electricity went off all over town. The dining room filled up over and over. There were candles on the tables and out in the kitchen, bending over in the heat. We had no use of the fryers or roaster and no water because our pump ran by electricity. The boys got milk cans of water from the hydrants down town for coffee and some dishwashing. Our stoves were gas, so the burners were crowded with water boiling for coffee, big fry pans cooking food that usually went in the fryer, more potatoes to mash by hand, and whatever we could heat or cook. We drooped, and the girls ran themselves ragged in the dining room. Doggedly we served till there were no clean dishes to put food on. The customers called it a picnic; we thought it a near disaster. But one good thing came out of it: the second payment on the taxes was assured. Coming into that unbelievable mess on Monday morning made us want to run the other way. But, with all hands on deck, things returned to normal, and we made believe nothing had happened. Once, when a robin flew into the transformer and knocked the current off, I didn't know it till the Fairmont truck driver knocked at the door downstairs. Looking at the clock I wondered why he was delivering at six in the morning, then discovered by my watch it was two hours later. Utility crews were called and luckily the things in the freezers and refrigerators hadn't started thawing. When lightning struck a tree and a branch fell across the wires near the road, we had to call the crew again to put out the fire and cut down the tree.

Our days were cut into pie-shaped pieces: the help with a third of the time with us; mine into pre-preparation, serving and cleanup, with a tiny sliver saved out for my morning walk with nature; and the leisure of a ride when we took the help home at ten or ten-thirty. Stanley had told me once, "We'll never have much money, but you'll never be bored." And I wasn't.

We weren't aware of being inspected, one summer evening, till the four men who had each ordered a different entree came out in the kitchen, showed us their *Mobil Guide* badges, and looked the kitchen and storage parts of the building over very thoroughly. But it was not till winter, when we got an excited call from Mary in Elmhurst telling us to look in the Parade section of the Sunday paper, that we found Samuelson's rated by *Mobil Guide* as one of sixty-four best restaurants in North America! In the guide we had a four star rating. Our home style, unadvertised Home Cooking had paid off.

Quirks And Quibbles

Everybody has a right to be himself, like Popeye, to be "I Yam What I Yam." It would be a pretty boring world if we were all perfect. I learned early, when I worked one summer in the early twenties, that unexpected quirks were highlights of one's personality. I remember waiting on table for a group of women one day. The hostess, who was entertaining at the luncheon, was really out to make an impression on her guests. We heard of her car and chauffeur, her summer and winter homes, her husband's profession, and her place in society. Talk flowed easily; the women were very congenial. Then, as I carried in the dessert, fresh raspberry parfait, and was about to serve her, she said in a carrying voice, "No, thank you. Raspberries are one of my idi-*oscracies*." I grabbed the tray and hustled back to the kitchen, so she couldn't see me laughing.

Before we enlarged the kitchen and ordered a custom built dishwasher (from a designer who must have thought he was allowing space for a hole in the wall), we had problems getting someone to dunk those heavy wood dish racks in the three rinse tubs. Stanley, in the cherry orchard daytimes with a crew of pickers, asked if anyone would be interested in dishwashing. Milton offered his services. He was, he said, a dishwasher in a cafe in Minneapolis every winter. So he came over from the camp on a Friday evening to be initiated into our ways. At five he appeared, hair slicked down, white shirt and pants clean though unironed. We furnished the apron. He worked steadily, but thought it his duty to entertain us. We were informed that up at Minneapolis the cafe he worked in was in the same building as a radio station. He was on the best of terms with radio entertainers, especially a girls' trio. He took them out to movies, he said, paid for their meals at the cafe, and bought them presents, silk stockings, perfume, and pearl necklaces. He tried hard to make a good impression on our Joyce, but she wasn't interested in his offers. Meanwhile, as the girls unloaded their trays of soiled dishes beside the sink, he drank the cream that was left in the little pitchers, and polished off the rolls left in baskets.

When he came in again Saturday he called me aside to say that he'd acquired a painful case of poison ivy, in a sensitive spot. Could he get some soda for it? I had better than that: Bob's prescription lotion. Bob was very susceptible to that horrid rash. That taken care of, he again made an effort to impress Joyce, and asked her to go to the movie with him. She sailed right past, not even answering, and he tried his wiles on the others, without luck.

On Sunday the rush was terrific, all of us going at top speed. No time for kidding around now. Poor Milton! He hadn't expected this kind of a workout, and the poison ivy was still torturing. Soiled dishes piled up at the sink, the girls clamored for more clean glasses, and Milton moaned and groaned. "This is enough to kill a man . . . Man can't stand this, he'll have a heart attack. There's no end to these dishes. Where do all those people come from? I can't take this."

Everyone tried to give him a helping hand, but our hands were pretty full, too. And the people came, and dishes piled up. No flip talk now about red silk stockings and perfume. No offers of movie dates or moonlit walks. When finally the crowd was fed and we had a chance to take our plates and eat in the lunch room, food didn't interest Milton. He pushed his plate aside and put his head down on the table and slept. The long day ended at last, and Milton limped home to the cherry camp, a worn and broken man. That was the last we saw of him, the last, too, of my son's prescription. Milton left for parts unknown next morning, taking the bottle with him, and we had to find another dishwasher.

We struggled through that year as best we could with a series of young men helping out. Then, before the next season started, a fast-talking salesman persuaded us to have a dishwasher built-in, custom-built for that room. The designer was anything but expert. The room was better ventilated now, and the machine, counter for soiled dishes, sink, and counter fit the space, but were far from adequate. During the wash and rinse cycles there was no place to hold the rack to fill for the next load of dishes. It was a slow process, though much better than the old wooden racks that had to be dunked by hand. But how often I wished we'd had that designer there for a week, to see the limitations for himself. Remodeling is for the birds, at least in restaurant kitchens. We suffered through mosquitoes, noise and workmen as the wall was torn out and kitchen expanded. I maintained all along that if a woman were hired to do the planning it would be much more efficient, but nobody heard me. It was better, but not step-saving convenient. And we managed.

It was the personal quality, not the building features, which helped us to success in our new venture. The restaurant provided the atmosphere; the supportive loyalty of the family — our own and the help who became family to us — provided the means to that success, along with the wonderful patrons who liked us and became good friends. There was quite a roster, the parade of help throughout the years. Alice, and Joyce, Doris, Helen, Florence, Viola, Lois, Corrine, Betty, Elda, Nancy and Sandy; almost all of them I had never known before. Now they were an essential part of our lives. There was some good natured teasing, sometimes some hurt feelings, but mostly we were concerned with helping each other, and pleasing our good friends and customers. For those hours when doors were open to hungry people we were an entity with one rule to follow: "Only the best at Samuelson's."

Godfrey, who came to us during our third summer, took over dishwashing duties, and stayed with us for twenty years. When he was fourteen, he was going home on his bicycle after attending a movie, and a drunk hit-and-run driver struck him. He lost a leg as a result. He joked about the artificial leg: "I take off ten pounds every night." He had a unique sense of humor. Ask him "Do you want to eat, Godfrey?" He'd say, "I don't think I'd taste very good." Kids used to say "Look, that guy walks just like Chester on 'Gunsmoke.' " He would come to work on his bicycle, and after we were all through work, Stanley would put his bike in the back of the car, and he'd ride along with us when we took Betty and Alice home.

Each season was different. The weather naturally affected our business, and cool rainy summers didn't bring out the summer people as the hot seasons did. Our employment list varied with the seasons; new faces appeared, new situations. We had all kinds: the efficient, concerned type who whizzed around as if on skates; the helper who had to do things her way, good but slow as molasses in January; the beauty queen with the bee hive hairdo; the charmer with the fabulous eyes and lashes; the boys helping Godfrey one summer, who broke so many dishes I finally threatened to make them pay for them; the boy who ran, never walked, to put kettles away or pile plates to keep hot on the warming shelf. We all loved the young girl who, when we'd ask if she wanted to cut more cabbage for cole slaw, always said, "I don't want to, but I will," quite a contrast to the girls who felt it necessary to make a dramatic appearance with the biggest piece of news or scandal they could gather. Alice said she often thought they made things up, just to have something to report. Family doings might be discussed, but we reserved the rights of privacy, although carrying voices didn't always protect secrets. The help had their outside interests, and Stanley and I had ours, too, though we had to forego them in summer time. But church, writer's club, classes, poetry round robins, needlepoint and crewel, Stanley's stamps and coins, welcome visits with our family and grandchildren all kept us from getting stale.

The first emergency call stands out in mind. A wedding party had prepared the food for their reception the day before, and the potato salad soured. Would we fix a hundred pounds of salad by two? Well, every burner on my gas stove was filled with bubbling potatoes, which I tested and removed to peel as soon as they were done. Alone till eleven, I had a start when Joyce came, and as soon as she had the dining room ready she pitched in, too, as did the boy who washed dishes, and Alice when she arrived at 11:30. The biggest pans we owned were filled with sliced potatoes. Diced onion, hard cooked eggs and salad dressing were fixed between Ziggy orders, and at two, when the men of the wedding party arrived, we had just finished mixing the salad and were topping with garnish. Made it!

About the time that we went on television, Channel Five, Green Bay, we got more and more interested in ethnic foods, particularly Scandinavian. We not only liked them, but enjoyed making the things we were able to master. Our own specialties were Belgian pie, kolaches, booyah, Grandma's shortcake, baked Alaska, pizza, chicken cacciatore, Martha's potato dumplings. But when Roger and Stanley made *klub* (blood dumpling) I cleared out.

I singed my hair at the big pizza oven we had for awhile. It was great for pies, except that the temperature in each oven stayed the same, as you couldn't set it back for one pie and up for another. I found that nobody was indispensable on the day when we were preparing for a rush evening and a catering job, and I was hit with a gall bladder attack and sent to bed. I locked myself out on the back porch when I took blankets out to air. Since I was alone, I sat, wrapped like a squaw in an Indian blanket, till Godfrey and Betty's husband, Lorney, came to paint and varnish, getting ready for Mother's Day opening and they let me in. And it would be hard to forget the years of the Packers' heyday, catering to pre-game parties and after-the-game celebrants. Good years, slow years, busy.

"Nothing but the best at Samuelson's" was our inside motto, and the parade of helpers through the years proved that. We may have brushed off a Pokey Polly, Sneaky Sarah, Giggle-bug Gertie, Snuggle-puss Sophie, the Beauty Queen, and the snippy girl who didn't realize her face looked like a dried apple, but all of those were compensated by the ones who came back, year after year, who pitched in through good times and bad. There was quite a parade of them: Alice, Lois, Godfrey and Betty, with us the longest; others, like Peter who persuaded us to have bus-boys, the six from the Bowen family: Aaron, Elaine, Danny, Fred, Annette, and Dick, who left us on graduation night. (He was a natural in the kitchen; I'd hoped he'd work with me at the serving table that summer.) All those boys on the clean-up staff: Jeff, Robin, Bill, Jim, Wayne, Bob, Greg, Doug, Paul, Tom, Howard, Roger, Dave, and the others who came and went. They were boys earning enough money washing walls and doing dishes to pay for hunting trips and some who became professional men and still claimed they liked us. Sometimes in summer George Hostlett, who made our signs, would take the whole crew on a moonlight ride on the *Lollipop* after clean-up. I can still see Elizabeth scouring the fryer and grill and polishing the serving table top. I remember Betty's vegetable or onion soup, which were so tasty, and her stories of Germany as a girl, and her family who helped us: Elda, Sandy, Dave, and once in a while, Lorney. Other memories: Lois' girls, Nancy and Sandra; Helen's ways with tying the bow on her apron, and being asked often if she was Mrs. Samuelson; Martha stepping in to help out in a tough spot, Corrine's lovely smile; Celeste, Margie, Lassie; Marlene asking if I'd like to go to the late show with her. Marion, Doloris, Joannie, Dorothy, Kathryn, Barb, June, Marilyn, Minnie, Esther, Joyce, and Alice, of course; and all the others who made the wheels go round. Through all the sad times, the glad times and the rough times, they stood behind us. Nothing but the best at Samuelson's.

The years went on. We all learned how to speed up the service, to step into another's place if need be. Our own form of assembly-line specialties helped build up the reputation for the restaurant. When the Four Star *Mobile Guide* Decal went up on the front door every person felt justifiable pride. The help rescued me when my holder or apron caught fire through my carelessness; they carried tea, coffee, or iced tea when we were ready to drop. We celebrated birthdays together, came early and stayed late. They were all indignant when one guest picked up the tip his brother-in-law left for the waitress. All of our quirks and quibbles were accepted. Our Sunday and evening family—Samuelson's.

"To Everything There Is A Season."

The only summers that were not relentlessly busy were the weather-plagued ones: cold, raw, dismal days, or rain that spoiled everyone's vacation. Then came Labor Day, and as if a curtain had fallen, the scene changed. But even that couldn't be counted on. One year, I remember most of the help going home for two or three hours till dinner time, while Elizabeth preferred to stay, doing my ironing, to keep busy. There was the year that Verna, Marian and I took the plane to Denver, and then on to Loveland to see our sister Vera, ill with muscular atrophy. We'd had a bit of a rush at noon. We left at 1:30, and that evening the help was hard put to care for the unexpected push. We were open five to nine weekdays; on Sundays from eleven on. Stanley and I tried to handle it alone except for Godfrey's help, till Saturday and Sunday.

Funny things happened on our way to our Forum. There were people who acted a little supercilious about our "one-horse" arrangement, who suddenly became impressed when important community figures came in. One night Stanley breezed into the kitchen where I was placidly putting out Ziggies and chicken in a basket, to tell me, "Eleven boxes to go in half an hour!" I sat right down on the floor and cried out, "I can't do it!" Godfrey looked at me, stricken, and said he'd help, and proceeded to set up the boxes with buttered rolls and souffle cups of coleslaw. The order was ready on time, and Father-dear said, "Why do you always say you can't? You know you're going to do it." Maybe, I thought, I'd better look on the other side of the mountain.

Wedding pictures pass before my eyes: Ruth's candlelight wedding, when Stanley burned a hole in his coat, backing too close to the candelabra while Herb Reynolds was taking pictures; Mary's wedding at the Sky Chapel of the Chicago Temple, with Stanley, Bob, and I making a flying trip down to be there, and the reception at the restaurant a week later; Bob and Lassie's wedding when he was home on furlough, the day before Thanksgiving, and Lassie forgetting to carry her bouquet when she walked up the aisle; that wonderful feeling of almost all of us together for our family Thanksgiving dinner the next evening.

The rush getting ready for those weddings was nothing like the day word came for Ruth and baby Douglas to meet Gil in San Diego, where his ship was to come in. Stanley and as many of the help as we could spare were out on the trial run of one of the L.S.T's built at the shipyard. We'd served a small group at noon and had to get ready for a larger one coming in that evening. Ruth managed to get a plane reservation from Chicago on, but there was no way to get there except by train from Green Bay. While she washed clothes and packed, Nancy took time from the dining room to push the baby in the stroller back and forth. Then nephew John, Vera's son, drove them to the train with just five minutes to spare. And, an hour after they'd left, the florist called that he had an order for anniversary flowers; what to do? Wait till she came back, or another anniversary, was all I could say.

Other weddings were memorable, remembered through the years. Our first wedding dinner, for my cousin Winifred. If only we'd started taking pictures of our brides, what a gallery we'd have! There were other celebrations: silver and golden anniversary dinners, the luncheon parties, Uncle Norman's birthday party for all the Samuelson relatives, when we finally managed to squeeze in a hundred and twelve people after serving more than that at noon. Will I ever forget the ones who filed through the kitchen to say hello, and Betty's desperate, "If one more person says "Poor Grace, I'll scream!" And there were the family groups who spent Mother's Day, Palm Sunday, Easter, baptisms and confirmations with us, and the high point of our year, our Thanksgiving dinner with the beautiful horn of plenty of fruits, vegetables and appetizers, and our own family get-togethers in the evening.

Once in awhile there was a bit of a flareup, as with the mother-in-law who thought she shouldn't pay full price because there was a lot of food left over from their family style dinner. She didn't see why we couldn't use that for the night serving, though we explained that that was to be a fish boil we catered. One Labor Day weekend a wedding party was cancelled out on short notice at the club and dance hall they'd engaged, and we sent food and help over to the church to be served there. The cost of one wedding got out of hand when the bride-to-be ordered identical dinners for eighty with us at noon and at a club and dance hall that night.

Her folks hadn't known she wanted it that way, and it took them three months to pay the tab. Another bride miscalculated expenses. She and her groom were paying for everything, but they didn't receive as much gift money as anticipated.

Crises came, too, when you least expected them. Stanley was taken by ambulance to the hospital with a suspected coronary on the day we had reservations for a hundred and five winter prom kids. The day was a blur, with his brother Roger taking me to the hospital, then back to the restaurant to receive deliveries and prepare. A salesman went out of his way to let Ruth and Gil know about Dad, since they didn't have a phone yet in their new home. Our wonderful, loyal help came in at ten and lined up the food we'd need. Ruth Pederson walked in at eleven with "Tell me what I can do." We automatically got plates and chicken-baskets to send out. Then the sharp ring of the phone at 1:15, Dr. Beck saying, "Grace, I just wanted you to know that Stanley's out of danger." I couldn't fill that last order.

Funerals weren't always sad times. We hadn't many funeral dinners to serve; most were at their churches. Sometimes more came to eat than attended the funeral. One couple, I remember, said, "It don't cost nothing; go home and fetch the kids so they can eat, too." There were some hard feelings when a woman who hoped to gain in a will had ordered lunch without telling the administrator, and, too often, there were family members who felt sad that it took a funeral for all the cousins and aunts and uncles, sisters and brothers to get together.

Gremlins pestered, too. When were were getting ready for a smorgasbord the milkman accidentally spilled a gallon of milk in the refrigerator. My yell, "Grab the fish molds," saved them from total destruction. Most of the men who serviced the restaurant were friendly and complimentary. On a rare occasion when two of the girls were having a heavy dispute, I was embarrassed and told the milkman that sort of thing almost never happened with us. He reassured me he heard lots worse, and more violent — even hairpulling at some of the places. Name calling was one of the things we simply did not tolerate, and one woman, who left us in a huff and went to work at a larger spot, was known to have informed those employees, "You never heard dirty jokes or nasty names at Samuelson's." Another girl, who walked out because Stanley asked her if she couldn't find something to do when the rest of us were going lickety-split, came back to ask to be reconsidered. But she'd cooked her own goose. Those were the only two

79

who ever quit. But there were a few who weren't asked to come back another summer; for various reasons they didn't fit in. There were a few accidents. Joyce got burned when someone told her to turn on all the burners of the broiler before lighting, and once a glass coffee maker exploded.

The Rube Goldberg job of plumbing at one sink was the nemesis of a new part-time worker; she fainted when she bumped her leg. I could have kissed Marion the day a pan of hot rolls turned topsy. Quickly she remarked, "I can see that you're going to have to start baking again," and the man waiting for his chicken boxes knew no floor strewn stuff would go into them. Grandma's oven flared out at her when she lit it to bake rolls one day, but the day was saved when Godfrey went downtown and got the pans, and I baked them for her, every Parker House roll in the pans were cut and folded over perfectly—my eighty-year-old mother-in-law never lost her baking touch.

When the heavy cutting board fell on my toe, turning it purple and causing swelling to twice the size immediately, I took off my shoe and hobbled round the corner into my bake room so the help wouldn't see me cry. Sore feet, callouses and corns, blistering heat at the broiler were occupational hazards I didn't get used to. Three extra pairs of shoes to change into were stashed in the corner. When I felt ready to pass out there were the blessed angels who brought me iced tea and kept me from real martyrdom.

On the night the broiler caught fire and the fire extinguisher was being put to use, one woman stupidly ran into the dining room and almost precipitated a panic by informing the patrons that there was a fire, and they'd have to wait awhile for their dinner. One of the few persons I truly disliked, she was a temporary employee, but she might have been permanent except for her tattling habit. The crunch came when she said our Bob had broken the thermometer in their pump shed. I pointed out he'd come down to eat breakfast late and that Stanley had taken him afterward to the Sunday matinee and called for him. Mrs. Know-it-all was never asked to help again.

Funny things, such as the customer who got black olive juice instead of iced tea, or stuffed olives rolling all over the kitchen floor when a jar spilled, just as a customer walked in, were commonplace. I learned I wasn't so smart when I tried making emergency chili, used chili sauce, and the order came back. I fixed salmon croquettes for our supper one Friday, and, when an extra flurry of customers came in and delayed us, we found salmon briquettes in the fryer. A whole roaster of chicken was left in the oven over-night, and had to be thrown out. One evening the hired man's "wife" stag-gered through the kitchen and down the length of the dining room. As she reached the rest room one man murmured, "She MADE it!"

Marilyn came bustling into the kitchen one Sunday night with the news there was a fox in the parking lot. It turned out that a pet fox belonging to some boys in Algoma somehow hitch-hiked a ride in a car of people coming to Samuelson's for dinner. Someone spied him in the parking lot, but he disappeared again, and when they stopped for a change of oil on their way home, the station attendant did a double take when he saw a fox under the hood. He kept the fox till they discovered who owned it; then the boys came to claim him and paid $3.00 for his keep.

Joannie told us of the fellow who lived down the line a way and told her, "Poor Sam! I feel so sorry for him. That big restaurant, and you never see a car parked out in front." She asked if he'd noticed that the sign in front read PARKING IN REAR, but that had escaped him.

Once I chased a man off the place. He was a religious fanatic who had been coming in at least every two weeks for years, and to whom I'd been giving change for his brochures, though I didn't agree with his principles. (He had come in the day that Stanley was in critical condition in the hospital, but the next time he didn't even inquire about him.) This day, when he got especially dictatorial, I told him about the close call, and said it was because of all the interdenominational prayers for Stanley that day that he got well. "Our road to God is not the only way," I said. He scoffed "Why you believe in the trinity; how can God be three persons?" "You get out, and don't you ever come back!"

Coping with being a grandmother wasn't as satisfactory as I'd have liked. I was too busy to be a "cookie Grandma," Ruth said, "but you're a full ice-cream freezer Grandma." There were few chances to have grandchil-dren stay with us, to tell stories to them my Grandma told me, and visits were infrequent. But all were loved as much as if we could see them daily.

When Stanley was initiated into the Shrine, Mary, Bob, and I went down to Milwaukee and shopped and went to a show. Getting back late we found this note from the help who had taken over that Saturday: "Dear Grace, phone us if you can't make it tonight so we know if we have to come early in the morning. —the committee." Could you find more loveable help than that?

Somehow health problems always surfaced in winter, and if there were operations or tests, I went to Green Bay for them all, including the gall bladder surgery that Stanley asked me why I never talked about.

I told him, "No, and you're never going to hear *my* story, either." The woman in the bed by the window related her struggle to swallow yards and yards of string so the doctors could see where to chip away the hardened deposit they removed from her throat. I heard that description morning to night to all of her visitors. I tried to shut it out by putting the pillow over my head, or turning on my radio. I couldn't turn away or get up as my own side hurt. I sympathized, but wearied, and when I learned that the elderly woman in the middle bed was found to have cancer, I cried. One time, when I was there for ulcer tests, my room partner beguiled everyone with intimate descriptions of surgery for female trouble. She had so many visitors they had to sit on my side of the room, too. I could have recited her ailments.

What I did think strange was that no matter how much they cautioned me to be careful when I got home, not to bend, not to lift, be careful of stairways, when I did get home there was a favorite aunt visiting, and I was the one who got meals and checked to see if she took her medicine. When I went back to the hospital for a check up, they considered me perfectly well enough to go back in the kitchen, lifting heavy roasters and kettles, standing on my feet or bending over the baking, or getting up at dawn to have enough pies ready for Sunday dinner. The only time surgery really frightened me was my thyroid operation—I hated to think of a knife so close to my jugular vein.

I had to cope with things when I was alone. Once I took the day's receipts and a crowbar up to bed with me. It always amused me when I answered the phone early and someone said, "Oh, did I get you up?" Once I said, "No, I was in the shower," and she said that was worse.

So, I went along, getting some fun out of each day and trying to keep my head on straight. I laughed when someone asked if I wanted a sweetheart (honeydew) melon, and when I could answer with a straight face, "Do you think we can *survive* this *endive*? When I discovered myself "breading" the chicken livers with powdered sugar, I laughed and saw some humor in getting an infection in my knuckle and having my wedding ring cut off. Once a meringue pie burned to a cinder while I went out to show Bob and Chuck where I wanted bulbs planted. Hearing we're "almost caught up" brought the immediate caution that those were dirty words-more customers sure to come. "No rest for the wicked," I'd hear, and, "I'll remember you in my will. I was poor once, too." Seasons came and went, but not without us. We could cope.

Who's In The Night?

All day long I had been at the serving table, filling up platters of chicken and ham for the Mother's Day crowd. From rising at dawn to cleaning up at night there was no respite. If there came a lull in the parade of customers taking Mom out to eat, we made good use of it by getting more food ready. The help ate whenever they had a few minutes; some of us never got a chance to sit down at all. More rolls, more pies, more chicken, ham, salad would be needed. Above all, there had to be plenty of spiced cherries on hand. Even though I was happy that the opening day of this season was successful, I was nervous, and I thought longingly of my bed.

We had gone to Florida just before Christmas, Stanley, Bob and I, the only time I was ever there. Stanley worked inspecting fruit and vegetables as a federal inspector; Bob went to high school, and I was "just a house-wife" for that time. I took a bus home in April, arriving in Green Bay in time for the arrival of grandson Paul. Then, the first of May, I came to Sturgeon Bay to open the restaurant for the season. Stanley stayed in Florida working till June, and Bob was in school. I was a little frightened of assuming full responsibility, but everyone was wonderful in helping.

So, with the kitchen and dining room in order again, the help went home and I thankfully carried the day's receipts upstairs. I felt secure, knowing that we'd taken in enough to pay the help and all the overhead expenses. After a warm bath, I crawled gratefully into bed, hiding the cash box and its receipts under the other pillow. In the morning I could get someone to take the deposit down to the bank.

Still, I lay there trembling, all thought of sleep or relaxation gone. A fine time for nerves, I thought. Whatever had got into me? I was exhausted, yet my eyes wouldn't close. What were those noises? Surely it couldn't be someone trying to get in? The doors were all locked, but people did know that I was here alone. I had left a light on out in the office, and in the kitchen, but this was such a rambling place; was that enough to scare someone off?

There was an unusual amount of traffic past the place that night. I heard a car roar up the driveway, taking a short cut through to the main road. Why were they coming through now, with the sign and the parking lot lights off? Little yipping sounds nearby; a dog barking. Was there someone prowling about? So many funny noises. The wind whiffed out the curtains at the window, making a pleading sound. Then it puffed out again and the ruffles struck the screen with a wheezing sound. I ruffled the pages of my magazine. I'd leave the light on and read; no one was likely to get in then. I could hear my heart pounding. This was silly! You're tired. Now get to sleep I told myself.

The clock down in the private dining room struck twelve. I had to get some sleep. From the grove down near the bay came the sound of an owl hooting, *who-o-o-o*, such an eerie sound! I shivered and pulled the covers closer about me. Then a snarl and a scream. I jumped right out of bed before I realized that it was the noise of two cats fighting.

That clock made such a grinding sound. It must need oil. I'll remember to do that tomorrow. (If I live through till tomorrow.) I turned over, punched my pillow, reached my hand under the other pillow to make sure the money box was still there. Then I turned again to reach the bed lamp. Maybe if I turned the light out I could go to sleep. Floor boards creaked (this place isn't *that* old!); the faucet in the bathroom set up a steady drip, drip, drip. I wanted to scream. The fog horn bellowed out its deep *oo-oo-oo*. Wind banged the louvres of the kitchen fans: slap, flap, bang! Another grinding noise; was it the motor on the big refrigerator? Or the pump? There were so many motors around the place. The grumble of the electric pump came up from below.

Suddenly I froze in fear. There was a low murmur, a squeak like the protest of the swinging door. I knew I heard stealthy footsteps moving across the dining room floor. There *was* someone down there! I switched on the light again, and looked wildly about for some sort of weapon. The only thing I could find was my hand mirror, over on the dresser. I reached over and got it, listening intently. Were those steps coming upstairs? If they were, I wanted to see him (or her!) first. I put one foot out of bed and drew it back as I decided against locking my bedroom door. I stepped out, cautiously, and padded to the door, reaching my hand out to turn on the hall switch. I steeled myself to look down. Nothing. The measured footsteps had stopped. What was he waiting for?

The chattering racket on the roof startled me even more. Could someone be trying to get in that way? My skin crawled with goose-pimples. Then, as a late driver gunned his motor when a pick up truck chugged by, I peeked out and watched the car's tail light as it turned down the driveway toward the bay. Shaking, I climbed into bed again. All was quiet. I felt myself relaxing. The next moment I screamed. That is, I tried to scream; just a little squeak came out. The heavy thud of some falling object echoed through the building. I sat up, clutching my covers and the hand mirror. The phone? I couldn't force myself to streak past that open stairway to the living room phone to call for help.

Silence. Then a soft tapping at the window. "Oh, God, Please—help me." Tender new leaves on the tree branches moved in the night breeze. I heard frogs croaking down in the hollow. A sleepy bird chirped, and the night owl answered. The telephone bell pealed, resounding through the room. I let it ring twice; then, realizing it was ringing downstairs as well for any intruder to hear, I crept past the open stairway to the living room and snatched up the phone. My voice stuttered a weak "Hello."

"I want two boxes of chicken to go," a mumbling voice told me.

"Sorry, we're closed," I muttered and slammed down the receiver. I sank down on the sofa, wrapped in the afghan. Eventually, I slept.

Daylight came. As I tiptoed cautiously down the stairs I heard those measured footsteps again. This time I knew what they were. The vibration from the refrigerator motor, down in the basement. At the end of the dining room a heavy hanging plant had fallen. Dirt and broken flower stems were strewn about, with pieces of pottery. I clutched the money box tightly. Mother's Day receipts and I were safe! But the telephone receiver was off the hook. Who's in the night? . . .

A Cook On T.V.

All ingredients are laid out on the table, 'ready-measured, waiting to be combined. The count down comes; one, two, three, four, and I repeat. The little red light comes on; the cameras roll. As if in a dream I hear: "We bring you now, Grace Samuelson, of Samuelson's Restaurant in Sturgeon Bay. Here she is: IN THE KITCHEN WITH GRACE. . . ." My heart in throat I manage "Hi!" with what, I hoped, wasn't a sickly smile. Hard to believe that for the next half hour this is MY show, in MY kitchen. All because I responded to a call from Channel Five asking me to demonstrate one or more of our specialities on the air for a series on restaurant cooking in the viewing area. The white and rye-graham rolls I made, along with the special pecan pie were what brought this on, since there were so many letters with requests for the recipes. So here I was, beginning what was to be three-and-a-half years of T.V. shows every Tuesday and Thursday. I was scheduled to make a finished product to show, to measure out and assemble all ingredients needed, drive with Stanley to Green Bay, and get home to help serve the dinner hour. Stanley not only had to see that he got me there safely and on time, but he gave the commercial, a plug for the restaurant, which was our pay for the job.

That day, September 17, 1957, was memorable to us in another way: our Bob was sworn into the Coast Guard, and left with his group for Alameda, California. He called, from the Palladium, where they waited for air flight time, just before I was to go on. Stanley and I were left with the empty nest syndrome.

The pay we got — doing the commercial for the restaurant — really was a good thing for us. It brought us customers from all over the viewing area, people who came to see the place, to eat, and to meet us in person. The help got a chance to meet those people, too. Sometimes we had so many folks that we dubbed it "visiting day at the institution." This was a wonderful chance to use the recipes I'd collected for years, and many folks sent me recipes, viewers, salesmen, and friends. In time we published two cook-books with the recipes I'd demonstrated; *In The Kitchen With Grace* and *Cooking With Grace*. A rush time, but fun time, too. We made many loyal friends with the crew and staff at the station, and with the customers who made our restaurant a frequent place to stop.

So, I kept on learning. Each show was a challenge, and in spite of the pressure, it was fun. The director, camera men, those who helped with the set, the men in the control room, all were friendly and willing to lend a hand. They all loved sampling the things I made, and would flock in from all over the station for something unusually appealing, rolls, dough-nuts, cookies, bread, soups, or cheese treats. Sometimes after the show was off, the cameras would roll again and pick up the whole gang eating and enjoying. We would pack up our box full of empty containers, leave word for someone to watch the pie, cake, or rolls still in the oven, and leave it for them. Then we were on our way home. Those rides to and from Green Bay were pleasant times, a chance for us to talk together. We didn't have much chance to be alone at the restaurant; Stanley was in the dining room and I in the kitchen during serving hours. His book work got done after we'd closed, and when we got home from taking the help home, I'd go upstairs to unwind, reading or watching T.V. till twelve or one. His accounts done, Stanley sat out in the office reading some of our book club books.

Sometimes I had guests for the show. There were the Cherry Blossom Queen, the Cherry Pie Queen, friends who showed how to make special Norwegian treats. Sometimes Alice or Betty came along. Once or twice I brought grandchildren. Diane, too, came up to the table with a cookie cutter and said, "Are we on T.V. now, Grandmaw?" The two Barrette grand-children had fun making faces on lollipop cookies. Our nephew Jack wanted to know if he'd have to be made up first. Sometimes I'd be asked to demon-strate some commercial product. How proud I was, after making the Robin Hood Lemon Jell Roll, to have the salesman tell me my cake looked even better than the one he saw at headquarters. Sometimes I had to write out my recipe card for the secretary to mimeograph while we were in the car. Doris Staidl, the consumer marketing agent, would come on Thursdays for her report and a demonstration. When it got to the busy season, I asked if she would do the Thursday show; one afternoon a week was enough during the summer season. Doris was fun to work with. She took over, too, when I took the train to Chicago to help Mary out after Diane was born October

4, 1957. Once, when I was making filled pancakes, I asked Doris if she'd roll them up when I put the filling in. Carefully folding them over, with a very straight face she commented, "And every one hand-rolled."

In the latter part of 1959 and the beginning of 1960, Marianne James had a daily show, and Doris and I became the cooking parts of it on Tuesdays and Thursdays. Marianne was a glamor gal, interested in beauty products, styles, and exercises, and getting a deep tan. I liked her. She wasn't high and mighty, and sometimes her questions about cooking or baking were pretty naive. She could laugh at herself when she told of a blooper she'd made. Demonstrating making an egg mask, and showing how to whip the yolks and then spread the beaten whites over that mixture to let it dry on your face, she had meant to say "Always put your eggs in the refrigerator; they'll whip up better." What came out, though, was, "Always put your legs in the refrigerator." She was surprised when I told her she'd really get more volume if the egg whites stood out at room temperature.

Marianne was fiercely loyal. Once I had come, bringing four pot roasts, one already done and the other three to be prepared in various methods. It so happened there was a greater number of commercials than usual that day, and they also wanted me to demonstrate a bread mix. The director, Joe Munn, approached me and said, "Grace, you'll only have two and a half minutes today." It drew sparks. I said, "Do you mean to tell me I've come fifty miles and brought four pot roasts to be on two and a half minutes?" Marianne flew into the office and informed them that if I didn't have more time she wouldn't be on at all. I got the extra time, and speeded up the bread demonstration so that I could show the four pot roasts in all their glory. When the cameras stopped Joe came up and kissed me, telling me that was wonderful; he knew I'd been upset. Another time he complimented me when a recipe didn't take as long to make as I planned, and I filled the rest of the two minutes talking.

Not that I was perfect every time. I sometimes left words hanging in the air while I peeked in the oven to see if the meringue was brown enough. I got used to "tours" of the station and had to be ready when I was asked why I never used animal fats, or "What you do if you're out of sour milk or buttermilk?" And, "Does it make any difference what brand of flour you use?" When I was making a salmon loaf one day I could see smoke curling up at the back of the stove. I looked over at the crew, but they were just watching what I was doing. There was a peculiar smell and the smoke got darker. I turned off the burner and turned the cream sauce, egg and salmon mixture into the loaf pan. Nobody knew that we almost had a fire. The new electric stove had been installed wrong. Once I announced a commercial too soon; the announcer wasn't at the mike yet. A couple of times I started talking without having my mike fastened on. Sometimes I'd say to send "a stamped self envelope" for a recipe. Once I set the oven for preheat without checking first, and a wax turkey inside soon was melting and smoking. Forgetting things was usually bad. One time it was the soda I'd left at home. One of the crew handed me a box from their cupboard, but when I went to measure it, all kinds of dirt, lint and rice fell out. They'd used that box of soda to demonstrate how well the vacuum cleaner picked up. The banana bread that day went in the oven without any leavening agent. When I forgot the frypan I liked to use for doughnuts, they brought me the one from the station, then couldn't find an electric cord. Whipped cream went to butter one day when I was showing a recipe for salad my sister-in-law had given me. Nothing to do but put it in anyway.

Every cook has a failure now and then. I couldn't be sure that the recipes I'd made at home would come out looking as good when made on a different stove. Most of the time they did, but once, making chocolate cream puffs, I heard Stanley say, "These don't look like the other ones did." (Luckily, not on the air.) They *had* flattened out, and I don't know why. I think the very worst moment was when Stanley was making his New Year's day oyster stew for me. The spoon he carried the butter on was hot, and he lost the butter on the floor. We had no more butter, so he scooped it up and plopped it in the broth, and I nearly died. There was no chance to say that we didn't do that at the restaurant, nor did we taste and put the spoon back as you see in some commercials. My bifocals tripped me up once—I thought I'd turned on the oven to preheat, but it was the wrong burner. A hot pan holder caught fire once, and one time I did a really dumb thing: dipped a plastic spoon into hot fat and watched it shrivel up.

Because of the show, and the cookbooks, I was asked to judge cooking contests, demonstrate for homemaker and other club groups, and even talk at a luncheon meeting a woman's club had at Samuelson's. All in all it was a different and pleasant experience, but truthfully, it was a relief, when the show had run its course, to be free, no longer a cook on T.V.

Rajah

Summer rush was over. After Labor Day most of the tourists and cottagers went home. The college students left a couple of weeks before that. We were open only in the evening during the week; Sundays were still busy days. We worked with a skeleton staff and seldom were we very rushed during the week, though there were still calls for boxed chicken. Clubs and church groups resumed their meetings. Now I was free to go to them, provided I had pies and rolls ready before leaving. The rolls stood in pans in the refrigerator, ready to go into the oven before serving time at five o'clock.

I was singing as I worked that September morning (the only time I dared sing was when I was alone; I'd lost my ability to carry a tune when I lost my tonsils) when there was a knock at the kitchen door. Even before I opened it I knew who was there. The rank odor of his corncob pipe preceded him. I laid down the strips I was ready to weave on my blueberry pie and went over to let him in. Rajah was a vagrant who had picked in our cherry orchard for a number of years. Stanley had given him, and his friends, Blackie, Chink, and Butch, permission to sleep in the barn. Each cooked his own meals down by the railroad track. They kept their own council as to the past; we asked no questions. Butch was a baker by trade. He came up to pick cherries every year on his vacation. Chink was versatile. He worked as a printer or a meat cutter during the winter months. Blackie, we knew, had been given his nickname after Boston Blackie. Rajah had worked in a carnival when he was young, as a snake charmer, therefore his name. Everyone liked him. For that matter, we liked them all, and trusted them. Until we opened the restaurant I'd always checked in the orchard and chatted with them from time to time. I found them interesting. Rajah's tall, sparse form cast a shadow on the screen door now. His grey eyes had lost their twinkle, and the puckish lips hung loosely. His face twitched, and he shook uncontrollably.

"Rajah! What happened? I thought you and Blackie had gone to Green Bay for warm clothes for apple picking. Are you sick?" I could tell what was the matter. Rajah, an alcoholic, had got through the whole season without drinking. Now he'd fallen off the wagon.

The slack lips trembled even more. "Well, Missus," he said, "Blackie and me took the bus down there Monday, but then we met a couple of buddies we used to know and they treated us to a drink. Can't remember much what happened, but I know we spent $85 over the bar, and woke up at the rescue mission, had to borrow money to come back on."

I told him to come in and have a cup of coffee. He shook his head, but asked if he could borrow some lemon extract.

Lemon extract! High alcohol content. No, I was not furthering his drunk. I said I never used it, and he wandered off, stumbling and shaking. Feeling sorry for him I went back to my pie making. What a shame. All his hard-earned money down the drain.

Once more there was a knock, and Rajah stepped inside. "Say, Missus, could I have a glass of water?"

"Sure, I'll get you one as soon as I put this pie in."

I handed him the glass and he set it down on top of the freezer, then took a bottle from his pocket . . . lemon extract! . . . and proceeded to pour the contents into the glass.

"Where did you get that?" I flared.

"Well, I know I shouldna done it, but I told Missus Utech next door you wanted to borrow some."

"Listen," I scolded, "we can't have you bothering the neighbors like that!" He wiped the moisture from his wobbly lips and hung his head. Stanley took him over to the hospital to get "dried out." He was very close to delerium tremens.

Two weeks later he knocked again. This time he looked much better. He pulled at his ear, shamefacedly, as he handed me a full bottle of lemon extract. "Say, Missus, would you mind giving this to Missus Utech? I haven't got the nerve."

Real Life Intrudes

The dining room was filled with customers, coming in after church or an early boat run, when Alice looked out from her place at the fryer to say, "Here's the cop's car. Wonder who he's looking for." We all paid little attention. The girls were bringing in orders, bus boys filling water glasses, Betty sending out trays of salads, and I was dishing up family style chicken.

Then, a couple of minutes later, the swinging door banged open and a policeman barged in carrying a large pruning knife. "Where's Stanley?" he asked officiously. "In the office, getting the cash box out," I told him, and pointed the way down the hall. "What on earth—?" He brushed past and disappeared, but was soon back. Stanley, cash box under his arm, led the way. They stopped just inside the kitchen door and conversed awhile. I was dying to find out what they were talking about and what the pruning knife had to do with it, but orders were waiting to be filled. The thought kept nagging me about Blackie coming over from the orchard early to tell me that someone had broken a window to the tool room in the barn in the night, and he wanted me to know he didn't have anything to do with it.

The cop drove off, and I waylaid Stanley long enough to find out that someone had broken in to Miss Losli's house, over on Shiloh Road, tied her up and badgered her for a couple of hours with that pruning knife as a threat, and then left before dawn, taking her money and a couple of Fruit Grower's checks.

It was hard to keep working while wondering what in the world had really happened, and what the customers thought about a cop walking through with that big knife. We couldn't turn the radio on for the noon news. It was too late, and besides, we'd never have been able to hear it with all the hubbub. We had to put it from our minds till the customers had gone; then we pumped Stanley for all the information he had.

The real shocker was that the robber had been picking at our orchard, and on Saturday afternoon Stanley had hired him and Blackie to tar the garage roof (a hot day: it took hot weather to be able to spread tar properly). The garage roof was just below the casement window in the kitchen, by the stoves, where Alice, Betty and I worked getting food ready for the Saturday night and Sunday crowds. It was hot in the kitchen, not as hot as it would be later on when the broiler was on all evening, but we felt sorry for those men out there, sweating as they mopped the hot tar over the roof. Betty brought iced lemonade and cherry pie out to them, and we called occasional words of encouragement down to them. They finished about four, and then we saw Stanley go over to the farm to pay the men off before he made the trip down for last minute supplies.

Sunday, when the news came over the local station at four, we heard: "A west-side lady had a terrifying experience last night. Miss Flora Losli, who lives on Shiloh Road, was awakened at two a.m. by a knock at the door. She turned on the light and was putting on her robe when she heard the sound of glass breaking, then a key turning in the lock. Then a shadowy form stood in the doorway. She ran for the telephone to call the police, but the intruder was quicker. Grabbing her roughly by the arm, he pulled her away, then yanked the phone right off the wall.

" 'Take it easy, lady,' a voice said. 'You won't get hurt if you do what I say.' She saw a young man, dressed in dark jeans and teeshirt. He had a vicious looking pruning knife. Just hand over your purse.

"The woman looked him over, noticing his slight build and the weapon in his hand. 'Aren't you ashamed of yourself, breaking in here in the middle of the night, asking for money from an old lady? Shame on you!' She shook her finger at him, defiantly. 'My purse is hanging on that doorknob. But all there's in it is five dollars and my Fruit Grower's check.'

" 'I told you wouldn't no harm come to you if you'd be good.' He reached for the purse and spat out a curse. 'Seventy-five-fifty! What a rip-off! Listen, you got more stashed away, I know that.'

"Miss Losli protested that was all she had, but she continued to scold the young fellow, and suddenly he turned on her. Pushing her roughly down in a chair, he grabbed the top sheet from the bed, tore it in strips, and tied her to the chair. He then searched the room, and she continued to lecture him. Frustrated, he threw himself into a rocker and lit up a cigarette, swearing under his breath. Then, failing to find anything more, he left the house as it was beginning to get light. Miss Losli managed to get herself loose, and called a passing car to notify the police. No trace of the burglar has been found, but it was learned he had been picking cherries at the Samuelson orchard, and had stolen the pruning knife there."

The tar on the garage roof still smelled hot. We were all a bit subdued and scared, thinking of what might have happened, feeling sorry for Miss Losli, who was a lovely person. I realized why Blackie had come so early to let me know about the tool room breakin. On Tuesday the *Door County Advocate* printed the story, and reported that Miss Losli had gone to stay with relatives. Stanley put new glass in the tool room window. The policeman brought the pruning knife back. There was only the black roof, and the chilling thought that it could have been the receipts of the day Mac was looking for, or Stanley might have been found in a ditch, his car and night deposit missing.

. . . . TWO ENGINES DEAD, PLANE, EIGHTY-FOUR SAFE IN PACIFIC DRAMA. Those were headlines in the March twentieth, 1963 issue of the Chicago *Tribune*. I had never thought that headlines might affect my life, but these certainly did. In our living quarters above the restaurant Stanley and I had been marking time till March nineteenth arrived. The restaurant was closed for the winter months; we'd had some free time to pursue hobbies, but all through the winter we'd been looking forward to this date. Our Bob and his wife, Lassie, and their two children, Stanley and Julie Ann, would be coming home from Hawaii, where they'd been stationed for two years. I was cleaning out cupboards. I wanted all my housecleaning done and the place in good shape for the time when the little family would come home. The weather the day before had been lovely, so it was disappointing to wake to frosted windows, swirling winds and driving snow. I consoled myself that at least the weather in far-off Hawaii would be much different for their take-off. And, certainly they wouldn't step into a blustery Wisconsin-type climate when they arrived in California! I found myself singing Mother's favorite hymn, "Count Your Blessings." As I scrubbed the shelves I kept thinking of that big bird, winging its way across the ocean.

At ten-thirty the phone rang. My sister Verna was calling. "Have you heard the news report?" she asked. "I hated to call you, but I felt you ought to know." A plane carrying military personnel from Hawaii was having difficulties over the Pacific. An engine had failed, and the pilot was forced to turn back, just before he'd reached the point of no return.

I ran into the living room and turned on the television, but the news flash was over. I ran to the radio in my bedroom, but heard only rock music and the "Hello Neighbor" program. I sank to my knees beside the bed. "Please, God," I prayed, "Please spare them. Please keep them safe."

I pounded on the floor, out in the kitchen, and Stanley, in the office below heard and came to the foot of the stairs to ask what I wanted. I screamed out the news and my fear, and he came up to see if he could get information. Another special report flashed on the screen. The crippled plane, having lost two motors, was on its way back to Hickham Field, a thousand miles away, and twelve hundred miles from Travis Air Base in California. There were eighty-four persons aboard including five military wives and nine children. The pilot had ordered all luggage dumped overboard to lighten the load. Escort planes would accompany them back to Hickham. Luggage! They had just bought new luggage for the trip and their belongings were at the bottom of the Pacific. I paced the floor, going between the radio and the television, trying to hear any new bit of news about them. Stanley kept repeating, "They'll make it. They'll be all right." I wrung my hands; where was my faith?

My mind was playing tricks. Kaleidoscopic pictures passed before me of the little boy we had waited so long for. Then I saw him, an earnest little seven year old just home from Sunday school, explaining carefully to me, "It's a good thing that God is Spirit, because if it weren't for that we wouldn't know about the law of gravity, and everything would fall."

Again the phone rang. It was Verna, saying: "I just remembered the poem we learned in school:

"We are lost!" the Captain shouted,
As he staggered down the stairs.
But his little daughter whispered,
As she took his icy hand,
"Isn't God upon the ocean,
Just the same as on the land?"
(The Tempest—James T. Fields)

Suddenly, I felt a deep calm. I *knew* that they were safe.

It was perhaps an hour later that the final message came. The Constellation had landed safely at Hilo Field, one hundred and fifty miles closer than Hickham. Emergency equipment standing by was not needed. A tire blew out as the plane landed, but there was no other damage, and the pilot said that the passengers had reacted calmly. The plane flew at 3500 feet, all under control and using less fuel. There was no injury to passengers or crew. Stanley's hand gripped mine, as we breathed a prayer of thanks. "UNDERNEATH ARE THE EVERLASTING ARMS."

Our long distance "welcome home" call came through later that evening. We learned then that they had not been on the crippled plane, but on the next flight. Bob had seen the passengers at the airport. Red Cross workers brought them in to replace the belongings which had been tossed overboard. Our prayers had simply been transferred to those flying back from the point of no return. How many thankful families were breathing easier now. His eye is surely on the sparrow.

The Customer Is Always Right

It had been a helter-skelter day. We were short one helper in the kitchen and this was chicken-cutting day. The boys waited for the truck to come with the iced chickens; today it was late. So the two boys sharpened their knives, got the trays and the cutting boards ready, then busied themselves stacking luncheon dishes and grinding the vegetables for Betty's soup, while listening for the sound of the truck coming up the driveway. Then, at last, the boxes were brought in, wooden crates with twenty-four chickens in iced layers, ten crates this time. Quickly the boys opened the crates and grabbed chickens. After their knives went down either side of the back-bone, they bent the breasts to remove the keel bone, and tossed the meaty pieces into water to be washed. Then Betty carried a tray full of the cut up chicken to the table to be floured and seasoned. Alice or I took over, browning the pieces in deep fat, getting them ready for the roasters. The livers were stored in gallon jars and refrigerated, waiting orders for chicken liver dinners. The giblets were put on to cook; later they would be chopped to add to the savory dressing. The necks and backbones went into empty cherry tins, and someone was always ready to pick them up for soup or booyah. Our daily deadline was approaching, but we were through with the cleaning up by the time the rolls had to go into the ovens and the roasted chickens brought out. There was time enough to set up the table for serving and to relish the first cup of coffee brought in from the dining room. The boys changed aprons and were ready for the dishwashing seige. We all drew a deep breath.

Almost immediately, the first customers were at the door. A family of five sat opposite the kitchen door; they ordered chicken family style. Two elderly couples sat down at the corner table. The dime store manager came in alone and sat near the door; she wanted a cubed steak. The dining room filled fast. Then Lois came in to tell us the Grouchies were in, with an-other couple. They really were tightwads and sourpusses, but they came quite often and usually with friends who footed the bill. They weren't our favorite customers.

That night they complained about the water, not iced enough. The rolls weren't hot (they'd just come from the oven). They lingered at the salad bar so long their soup was cold and they sent it back to be reheated. The reservations were coming in now. We hurried to pile the golden brown chicken high on the platters, and to send in the creamy whipped potatoes, silk-smooth gravy, and dressing oozing savory odors, along with the steaming vegetables, proud of our quick service. In two minutes Lois was back, her face stony as she carried in a platter of chicken, hacked and torn. "They said it must have been warmed over chicken," she said. "He carried it halfway the length of the dining room. Said they didn't want that kind of stuff!" Everyone in the kitchen was up in arms. *How could they say it was reheated?* If we hadn't been so tired it might have been funny. I filled another hot platter with chicken and, as Lois carried that to Mr. Grouchy, the people at the family table called, "Ours is delicious; anyone can tell it's freshly roasted." The older couples called out, "Ours is wonderful, such flavor!" Mr. Grouchy simply glowered and kept loudly proclaiming what beautiful chicken they got in Florida at the Mall. His wife agreed, all the while eating as if she enjoyed it. When the check went in the other couple paid the bill, and Grouchy told them, "You don't need to leave a tip for the girl. You'll never come again, anyway." My Irish was really up by that time, and I told the girls, "If they do come in again you can tell them Mrs. Samuelson said we don't care to serve them." But even in that ultimatum I was foiled, because they were part of a group one of our oldest (and most loved) customers brought in the following Sunday after church. And it was Mrs. Grouchy who suggested they order chicken family style. She did duck her head and refused to meet Lois's gaze; we knew she felt cheap.

Because those folks were rare birds, we put the insult from our minds. Other customers were happier company. We sharpened our sense of humor and kept going. Peter came into the kitchen choked with laughter one night, telling us of the two little old ladies who came and sat down with three other elderly women and said, "Fancy meeting you cats here!" There was the couple who looked over the menu and said as they left, "Can't be very good; doesn't cost enough." There were the people who asked for a drink and left because there was no bar, while the Catholic priest told us, "It's good to be able to eat in a place where a drunk's not breathing down your neck." If people telephoned about drinks, I told them to have a cocktail down town before coming out. I remember, when we opened, we kept hours from eleven a.m. to two a.m. On several nights, too weary to stay up longer, I went upstairs at 1 a.m. One night I was roused from slumber by loud singing and piano playing from the private dining room. I stumbled down in my housecoat to find one drunk cooking hamburgers while the overflow from the tavern belted out their not-exactly-Sunday-School songs. A couple of sessions like that and I made my point: eleven p.m. was late enough to stay open.

We got used to the questions: "Is your soup greasy?" "Does the dessert come with the dinner? Then, I'm going to eat pie if I bust." We weren't fond of the "well done" steak orders, and hated to see customers douse a good steak with catsup or A-1 sauce, but that was their privilege.

"Are the rolls hot?" "Is the pie fresh today—I can't eat yesterday's pie." (We wondered what they did at home.) "Is your ham salad sandwich made with Spam?" "Is the fish boned?" "How many pieces of chicken do you get on a plate?" "Can I get a child's portion? I don't eat much." "I'd like a spaghetti plate with chicken dressing on the side." "Can I have sweet potatoes on my shrimp?" "Apple sauce on my mashed potatoes?" "Do you use lard or vegetable shortening in your pie crust?" "This grilled cheese sandwich is scorched; no, you needn't bring it back. She'd probably do the same again."

Four ladies in the lunch room complained their ham plates were cold. "They were hot when I carried them in," said Elaine. "I suppose you stuck your finger in them to make sure," one sneered. "Can't see why you don't make lemon meringue week days. Shall we take the pecan or cherry?" "I'm on a diet—just give me a ziggy cheeseburger and onions. Then I'll have that fresh strawberry pie, ala mode." Elaine confided to us that what she'd like to give them was a copy of Emily Post. I realized from our experiences how much a kind word or two meant to the dining room girls, and learned to make a special effort to be civil when I ate out. Not long ago I heard a woman in an out-of-town restaurant bawl out the waitress because she had reached across to set her plate down (there being not enough room to get around her). "That's what you can expect in a place like this!" she snapped, and I wanted to pat that waitress and say, "It's all right."

We were amused at the woman who asked us, "Do you wash your birch trees?" Lois kept an eye out for Pocketbook, who not only took home the rest of her family style chicken, but relishes, rolls, salads, spiced cherries and vegetables. It all went into little plastic bags she carried in her purse.

One family bragged that they'd started taking their two boys out to eat when very young, so they'd be accustomed to it. They surely were! When that family left, the floor around their table was a disaster area, to say nothing of the nearby ones whose occupants had been the targets of bits of rolls and relishes.

While the general run of customers more than made up for those few weirdos who rubbed us the wrong way, we couldn't help remembering the trio who pushed their way into a reservation filled Mother's Day crowd, then insisted on steaks instead of our limited menu of ham, chicken and turkey on that day. "This is pork, not beef!" snarled the lady (?) as she poked a forkful of the meat at Stanley. "Lady, if you can find any pork in this place, I'll give it to you," he told her. But Doris was almost in tears while trying to accommodate them. Another time, when we had opened especially at noon one fall for a club group, four women from Manitowoc stopped. "They sent me in to see if you wouldn't take us" the husky woman told us. "Please—we'll take what you're having for the group." So we said yes, and were thoroughly disgusted at their criticisms, especially when dessert came, pumpkin pie with a ruffle of ice cream on the edge. "What's the matter? Did you run short of ice cream?" our pleader asked. That was one time I almost took off my apron to go in and state what I thought of them. And I very nearly did one time when a night club owner from Green Bay breezed in and loudly proclaimed everything served and the method of serving inferior. Every worker in the place was up in arms, ready to show her the way out. They kept muttering all afternoon, "Sourpuss! Beef-Crab! Too dumb to know that there's nothing but the best at Samuelson's!" Loyalty personified. Still, four or five lemons in twenty-three years wasn't a bad average.

But the good ones! There were the cottage people who became staunch friends, not because they praised us, but because they liked us. We loved them and enjoyed our conversations. They came for meals, in groups or in twosomes. They came to get chicken to go, or spaghetti or perch, pies to take back for their city freezers. Tourists stopped by, telling of friends from home who had recommended us. Stanley had lengthy discussions with many in the dining room and because he was well read, he had good rapport with them. We shared jokes with our kitchen customers: the man who was sent down town to get some broccoli and came home with a cucumber—"That's green." There was the family of three who came year after year on vacation, and who, on our thirty-fifth wedding anniversary came to the kitchen door and serenaded us! And the folks who seemed to enjoy our visiting grandchildren as much as we did. Yes, customers are ALWAYS RIGHT!

The Customer Is Always Right
P.S. — Revenge Is Sweet.

Her phone calls always reached me when we were busiest. One day she informed me that they were having company, about eight couples on Sunday evening. She'd like us to cater part of the meal and send a girl to wait table. She'd take care of the meat; we could deliver escalloped potatoes, green peas with mint, clover leaf rolls, raw relishes, and a large cheesecake with cherry topping. Wow! on our busiest day, and one waitress short. But we managed, and Lois and Stanley went over at five to supervise. The meal wasn't ready till eight, however. Her preparation of the shish kebobs was made on tiny rotisserie table grills, and took forever. Borrowed linen, silver and crystal made a heterogeneous assortment on the tables. The guests stuffed themselves with dips and canapes till dinner was finally served. (Funny, we thought, with all their money.)

The next summer her husband was having guests from Israel and it was beef stroganoff she ordered, along with noodles Romanoff, hot rolls, watermelon basket with fresh fruit salad, relishes and twin chocolate almond tortes frosted with chocolate whipped cream. I worked from 1:30 on Sunday, carving the melon basket, keeping an eye on the stroganoff, adding the sour cream at the last moment, trying to pacify two of the help who argued over who should fix the relish tray and who frost the tortes. Chicken box orders coming in between didn't speed us up. She called the next day to say everything was wonderful, but only fifteen instead of thirty-five had come. Before she could ask me to take the extra food back I told her I had an order to do and thanked her for telling me it was good.

A year passed before she reported that some of her husband's business associates were coming. This time she wanted me to buy a twelve pound turkey and roast it, make two large Jell-o molds and four cherry pies. Oh, yes— "send a large bowl of whipped potatoes and just the juice from the turkey; carve the turkey, please." At ten o'clock on Saturday the Jell-o molds were made, pies out of the oven, turkey in the roaster, when her call came.

"I got out from under the dryer to tell you. We've decided to take the guests out instead, so you don't need to send the food." I almost went into shock. "Why it's all being prepared now!" "Oh, well, you can use it anyway—I got out from the dryer to tell you." I was so angry I could hardly speak. "I suppose I'll have to," I managed to croak. The salesman who was waiting to take my order for Monday's delivery told me I should send the bill for all that food to her husband. I was foolish enough not to do it. One thing, she'd never get another order from my restaurant!

Two years went by before her dulcet tones came over our line again. "Mrs. Samuelson," she purred. "I was looking up your recipe for stroganoff in your cook book. Remember you made it for me and everyone raved about it? I've given so many girls that recipe." She was buttering me up; I wondered what she thought she'd get? "I'm having my golf club girls over on Tuesday, and I'd like you to make two of those lovely sandwich loaves you do so well."

There must have been a special little devil inside me. I answered very sweetly, "Oh, I'm sorry. I couldn't possibly do it Tuesday. I'm just too busy with my baking. Sandwich loaves take so much time to do."

"Oh, they don't take long."

"No?" my voice was really cold now. "I make all my own fillings and that takes an hour alone. Then the spreading and the cream cheese frosting and decorating take at least another hour. I'd never have pies ready for noon." I ached to ask her if it didn't take long, why didn't she do it herself? I hung up, not even saying I'm sorry, and left her sputtering.

It was a long wait, but it was worth it. I had done the inexcusable, refused an order. I felt mean, yet, revenge is sweet.

Last Move

The door of the moving van yawned wide and hungry. Like industrious ants the blue garbed workmen moved down the outside stairway, carrying the last of the furniture and the memorabilia from our living quarters over the restaurant. Nearly twenty-five years of family living was eased into the van's interior: mementoes, memories, and mundane artifacts. I watched as the huge boxes of treasured books, which I found so little time to read, the pictures, the hand work, and the well worn furniture were fitted like parts of a jigsaw puzzle into the van's maw. The memories *we* had to carry away. Now just the painted walls, bare floors and empty cupboards were left for new owners to fill. We recalled a number of farewells: our young folks leaving one by one to new homes, jobs, or the service; final farewells to the two grandmothers who had lived with us for a time; the comings and goings of nine grandchildren. Why did I have a lump in my throat? I knew the time had come to go.

I recall the moments snatched for leisure activities, borrowing time from pressing work hours to just be me, to reach for serenity; finding time to worship and pray by way of radio, when others were free to attend services; stealing little islands of time to devote to my family, to stroll in early morning to restore my soul. There were my small efforts at gardening: the lilacs I planted each spring for fourteen years, which thrived but never blossomed; my iris; the delphinium I so proudly raised from seed, as I did the columbine. It was a tug, leaving them, but it was time. Who was it said, "Time stays; we go."?

Disconsolately I followed the men downstairs to the restaurant proper. Here, only our personal belongings would be taken: the antique clock Stanley got at an auction in Iowa; my needlepoint picture made, in Depression years, of yarn ravelled from mitten ends; the family china, collectibles, and the few cherished heirlooms that found a haven in the van's big belly. There was also Stanley's stamp and coin collections—what was left of them—from the little closet he'd built under the stairs. They stirred memories of our dream of visiting Bob and Lassie in Hawaii, on the proceeds of selling the collections, but they weren't worth enough.

Filing cabinets, jammed with years' collections of recipes, menus, clippings. I've always thought I'd like to assemble pioneer Door County recipes. One of the files in Stanley's office had most of the letters we received from T.V. viewers, and Stanley had snapshot albums, the cherished memorabilia of our twenty-two years' stay. How could one pack away the memory of early dawn to late night labor, enveloped in heat and perspiration, as the racing hands of the clock ticked off the years; the joy of labor, bound together in fun and caring; or the years of Stanley's Parkinson's disease, when he could no longer fill the coffee cups or visit with the customers? As we left could we take with us the powerful feelings of stress and strain, the drive, the challenge, worry, dreams, pride in achievement, friendly affection, all the things that made up our dreams of a lifetime?

Last stop, the basement. Here some things would wait for the garage sale the next day. Stored furniture was gathered and packed. So, too, were the reminiscences of younger days, our plans to assure retirement years in comfort and leisure. We laid those plans aside, as the bogey of ill health appeared, along with the dread of being put on the shelf. It was the end of an era. What we had left was memories, friends, family, and a chance to make our golden years useful.

The van was loaded; the huge doors locked. We took along all we'd have room for in our new surroundings, all that we were entitled to. The lonesome fireplace, the view we loved, the birch trees and the song birds, my walk for serenity to the little family cemetery—all this we exchanged for a glorious view on the bay with life and activity, lights and ever-changing reflections. The concrete block building that Stanley planned and helped build, which housed love, laughter, labor, sorrow and joy, would bring a new life to other occupants. We already missed our long-time patrons and new-found friends, our employees, so loyal that they became family, too. These we left behind. How much is left! How much we take! Silently we followed the van. It was "Good-by, Samuelson's." WHY DID I FEEL SO HOLLOW?

A YEAR
FROM THE PAST

January

No matter how folks celebrate the New Year, they all seem to be glad the old year is over. Hope springs eternal that the New Year will bring a change for the better.

At the turn of the century, the New Year celebration for many folks centered around the Watch-Night services held at the various churches. My sisters and I looked forward to those services and to the parties that followed them, for they were a once-in-a-year opportunity to be out so late at night.

We set out, all bundled up against the zero weather that had etched the kitchen windows with scrolls, palm fronds, ferns, fairy castles, and oriental scenes. Outside, the snow sparkled like diamonds, and the bare limbs of the trees were coated with an opalescent glow. We got into layer after layer of warm clothing: long underwear, warm black stockings, flannel bloomers, petticoats, and garter waists. Then, wool dresses, sweaters, chamois skin vests (Papa, whose days of sailing as a young man had made him adept with a heavy canvas needle, had sewn these for each of us), black cotton tights, high laced boots, coats, scarves, stocking caps, and heavy wool mittens. It was a wonder we could stand up!

Outside, we marvelled at the stars and the gorgeous display of northern lights, as we plodded along, walking in the road if the snow was deep, following the sleigh or cutter tracks. The seven or eight blocks to the church seemed a short distance, even though our toes tingled through their covering and our fingers numbed inside our red mittens. Reaching the church, we stomped off as much snow as possible and removed our outer wraps and overshoes. We were always told that wearing rubbers indoors was bad for the eyes. We looked around to see who among our Sunday School friends we could sit with. Usually we would find the Pereson girls: Agnes, Amy, Mina, and Caroly, and Hattie Maples, who with her family had walked across the frozen bay. Dorothy Wilson would be there, too. Her mother,

Nettie, would most likely present an "elocution exercise" during the program. We enjoyed Watch-Night services — the social time in the church parlors, the lunch and hot chocolate that the ladies of the church provided, and, of course, the prayers for the year, as the town clock struck twelve. We even liked the walk home, anticipating the good that was to come in the New Year. From other churches, all over Sturgeon Bay and Sawyer, families wended their way home: the sleepy children stumbling along or being pulled on their sleds, the grown-ups mulling over problems and blessings of the year.

New Year's Eve, before we left for the service, had generally been spent writing out our resolutions for the year to come. Sitting around the dining room table, we listed the self-improvements we planned to make. Sometimes we would read them to the family; more often, however, we kept our own counsel and hid the list in the diary we started afresh each year, vowing to write daily. And we did write regularly for a couple of weeks or so, but soon the writing dribbled off to brief mentions of weather or company, and, as we found more interesting things to occupy us, the diaries, and the resolutions, were set aside. Nevertheless, it was cozy, on December 31st, sitting with the family and anticipating bigger and better things. Papa told us that even if the resolutions were broken, at least we had made an effort, and that was what counted.

New Year's Day we always took down the Christmas tree and packed away the ornaments. Lovingly, we wrapped our favorites, packing them gently, to be taken up to the attic and stored alongside the cistern. The tree was carried out, set in the snowbank, and hung with crusts and suet for the birds. We girls swept up the pine needles, and then we all set to cleaning our drawers and straightening up our books, writing materials, and school supplies. We *had* to be organized, because we felt that what we did on New Year's Day would be what we did all the year.

In those days, we had no radio or T.V. commentators to sum up the important events of the year and their effects on the country. The *Door County Advocate* listed the top stories in Door County, and we'd hear oldsters talk of hard times and high taxes, murmuring, "Don't know what this world is coming to, anyway." We went out sliding or skating in the afternoon, full of roast beef and apple pie. When we came in later to warm up, we'd get out the Christmas games and books, read the *Farmer's Almanac* or the serial running in the *Youth's Companion*, or cut out paper dolls or the Campbell Kids from The *Ladies Home Journal* or *Woman's Home Com-*

panion. We never heard of January blahs. We took it for granted that there'd be blizzards, with perhaps a thaw, but that was a Wisconsin winter, and you couldn't do anything about it.

I'm not sure if Januaries were colder and snowier then than they are now, but lacking many of the conveniences we've come to depend on today, the weather seemed to play a bigger part in our lives. Many mornings, we awoke to find the thermometer outside the kitchen window registering 20 degrees below zero (it was hard to read the numbers, though, with the frost so thick on the window and storm window). We heard Papa shaking the grates of the coal range in the dining room, and then the rumble of coal from the scuttle, as he filled the hopper.

We would snuggle down underneath our wool comforters for about five minutes more, until the faint waves of warmth wafted up through the open register over the range. But there was little comfort to be gotten from this source, and so we three young girls, in outing-flannel nighties and crocheted bedroom slippers, would grab the chilly piles of clothes on the chairs beside our beds and hurry downstairs to dress behind the kitchen stove, where Mama was already preparing Papa's favorite winter breakfast of buckwheat pancakes.

There was no dallying or daydreaming on these frigid mornings. On went all those layers of clothes. A speedy wash-up with water from the reservoir in the stove, and there we were, as expected, at the breakfast table by seven.

My sisters and I didn't care for the buckwheat cakes, made, like sourdough bread, from a "starter." Instead we would have oatmeal that had steamed in the double boiler on the flat plate at the back of the coal range all night. Usually Mama had toasted half a loaf of bread in the wire rack on the stove top. The toast, buttered and stacked high on a plate, came from the oven hot, soft, and delicious. Our baby sister chewed on a small piece as she banged her spoon on the high chair tray, waiting impatiently to be fed her cereal and mug of milk.

Smoke from a neighbor's chimney rose straight up, indicating clear, cold weather, and Papa, as he left for work, would admonish us to "bundle up good." He carried his lunch in winter, because that long cold walk over the toll bridge was too uncomfortable to permit him to come home at noon. Mama was already at her daily work, setting up the ironing board and heating the sad irons, mixing up the bread "sponged" the night before, or stirring up a batch of cookies to be baked later.

111

We didn't have to be at school till nine, so we each had chores to do—bed making, dusting, washing breakfast dishes, carrying the pitchers of milk and cream left from breakfast down to the cellar, and at the same time, bringing up eggs from the crock of jelly-like substance called water-glass, vegetables, canned fruit, or anything else Mama would need. It was our job to keep the woodbox filled and carry in the kindling and extra scuttles of coal so we didn't run out before Papa got home from work.

Two of us carried in a pail of water from the pump, which Papa had thawed out before he left. He also had carried out the stove and range ashes; wood ashes were saved for soap-making and coal ashes to spread on slippery sidewalks.

We filled the big tea kettle and set it over an open burner to boil. Winter usually brought some epidemic, and Dr. Kreitzer always recommended boiling the drinking water for at least 20 minutes. Several glass jugs of the "pure" water were stored on shelves on the back porch, which we called the "storm shed" in winter because it was boarded up for protection from wind and snow.

It took some time to "bundle up" as Papa instructed, but finally, we pulled our stocking caps down over our eyebrows, wound our scarves twice around the neck and pulled them up to cover our noses so that only our eyes showed, donned two pairs of home-knit mittens, and stepped out into the cold.

Papa always said I went off to school "like a shot out of a gun." Never late, but never early, either, I timed my departure so that I would be on time if I ran all the way. But in sub-zero weather, we all went together, keeping close for warmth, and we had to allow enough time to be able to get all those wraps hung up before the last bell rang.

Struggling through waist-high snow down the alley behind Hutto's, we plunged into the sleigh tracks on the road and groped our way past Johnny Feurenstein's house down the hill, ducking in the biting wind and trying hard to walk in the steps made before us. By the time we reached the Dana house, I was often in tears, and the moisture froze on my lashes. White frost climbed up our scarves where our breath came through and dusted the edge of our stocking caps.

Only two more blocks to go now, with the snow creeping up under our skirts and inside our tights. We persevered, however, and finally reached the school, where we stamped the snow off our overshoes and brushed it from our coats as best we could, and then headed for our individual cloakrooms.

Some of the kids had white spots on cheeks, noses, and ears. Often chilblains burned our feet, and then we thought of Mama, coming in from hanging out the clothes, rubbing red and near purple fingers and trying to "warm" them in cold water.

In this frigid weather, Mama packed lunches for us, even though we had an hour and a half at noon. We loved that part of the cold spell, eating leftover meat loaf or cheese on brown bread, and then ginger snaps and a big red apple. Sometimes we stole out in the cold, down to Schmidt's Bakery to relish "bought" goodies, jam-filled sweet rolls, jelly doughnuts, or crullers (we called them "crawlers"). If we had a penny or so earned from running errands, we plowed through the two and a half blocks of drifted sidewalks to L.M. Washburn's grocery and dawdled over the wonderful choices in the candy counter. Jawbreakers, "dumb-bells," little mixed jelly beans, stick candy with a gold ring on it, licorice sticks, horehound drops, rock candy, peppermint and wintergreen drops, taffy kisses, maple sugar hearts, lemon drops—what decisions!

In Miss Jenkins's Primary Room, I wrote my sums on a slate and learned to read from a Beacon Reader. Papa had had Miss Jenkins for a teacher, too, when he lived in Egg Harbor. Some years later, when she died, school was closed the day of her funeral, and all the children and teachers marched to the cemetery, followed by many businessmen and housewives, all former pupils.

By the time four o'clock came, our wraps were in a fair state of dryness. We didn't need urging to "come straight home," where we knew we would be welcomed by the smell of fresh bread, vegetable soup simmering at the back of the stove, apple dumplings, pie, steamed raspberry puddings, custardy bread pudding, or devil's food cake. We hustled through evening chores, did our homework, and helped drill each other in spelling and multiplication tables. By the time Papa got home, it was dark.

Sometimes, if it wasn't too cold and if there was a moon, we might be allowed to go sliding, after supper dishes were done. As there were no cars, and the horses were never taken out at night except for church services or sleigh ride parties in the country, sliding down the road was permissible. With Flexible Flyers and other sleds—a couple of the neighbor boys even had bobsleds—we would start down Minor's hill with a run and a jump and fly down the road. If you gained enough momentum, you could sail right on down to the ice on the bay. The walk up the hill wasn't as speedy, but we didn't mind that. Fun and comradeship prevailed, as we laughed and hollered, slid and climbed till our mothers began calling us in at 8:30. Spent and happy, we hustled into the cozy warmth and lamp-light, relishing the hot cocoa and cookies Mama had ready for us. We weren't allowed to go skating at night till we were "big kids," but when we finally achieved that privilege, it was ecstasy, skimming along the ice on Market Square, sometimes gathering up nerve enough to play "Crack the Whip."

Many years later, the Great Depression found me and my own family living in the old farm house on the hill, surrounded by an orchard. The house belonged to Grandpa and Grandma Samuelson, so we were able to live there rent free. The original log part had been sided over and an L-shaped addition built on one end, including a huge kitchen, pantry, and entry, which were a step up from the living-dining room. Our girls used the pantry as a playroom after Grandpa and my husband, Stanley, built cupboards in the kitchen.

In January, that kitchen was so cold during sub-zero weather that the mop boards wore a permanent coat of frost. We moved the beds into the log rooms, which had window sills that were 18 inches deep and were a perfect spot for my plants. They bloomed profusely there, hiding the frost on the windows. The first winter I ironed with sad irons and brought our washing over to Herlache's to do. Then Stanley wired the house, and we had a radio that entertained the girls with stories by "Uncle Mal" and "The Singing Lady." When I wasn't knee-deep in writing-contest entries, I was elbow-deep in bread or roll dough, or making peanut butter cookies or whipped cream cakes. The Dutch oven was in almost continual use, and cooking smells filled the air most of the day. We ate well, in spite of the scarcity of money. A side of pork and a quarter of beef (purchased in trade) had their own "freezer compartment" upstairs, on a long table covered with butcher's paper and dish towels. We had our own chickens, capons, and eggs, and the trap door to the basement led to barrels of apples, vegetables from the garden, and canned fruits and relishes put up in the summer.

We were lucky to be healthy; no longer did you hear of chilblains, catarrh, la grippe, or quinsy. Our children had been vaccinated for small-pox, diphtheria, typhoid—what a blessing!

And so we lived happily through January and eventually, the frigid days passed. It may have been rugged—but it usually was fun, too!

February

Often there was a thaw in January, and then February would settle down to more snow and ice and cold winds, but we never seemed to mind as much. It's a short month and was always enjoyable because of all the holidays. Patriotism held sway. It was a month that made history come alive and gave us an excuse for parties, programs, and the like.

I was in first grade when we learned that our flag now had 48 stars. New Mexico had been admitted to the union on January 6, 1912, and then Arizona on February 14. We talked about what a wonderful country we lived in and how fortunate we were to live in the "Land of the Free." We were also instructed that, like the lives of great men, we should leave behind us "footprints on the sands of time."

The teacher used to have us put our heads down on our desks to rest awhile after we came in from recess. Then, as she moved up and down the aisles, laying a light hand on our "sleepy" heads, the delicate aroma of her talcum floated by. That was the grade where I learned which was north and which was south.

In those days, our holidays weren't juggled around so that they'd always come on a Monday. We looked forward to the various days and made much ado in preparation.

Groundhog Day wasn't a holiday but a conversation piece, and we'd speculate before and after as to the six more weeks of winter. There would still be time for sliding, ice skating, games of fox and geese, skiing, and the guilty pleasure of sneaking that forbidden hitch on the bobsleds that came into town.

During those special days at school, we read stories of famous heroes and statesmen. We learned about Edison and his inventions—his birthday was the eleventh. Next came Honest Abe, best loved of all the famous. We heard the stories of how he walked miles to return a penny he'd been overpaid, of pulling a pig out of a mire, and of how his simple speech at Gettysburg surpassed the two-hour oration of Hale, and stories of how he freed the slaves and struggled to unite a country divided. For our Lincoln booklets, we drew log cabins and rail fences, and we cut silhouettes of his familiar head. We sang "Tenting in the Old Camp Ground" and "The Battle Hymn of the Republic." At home a jelly roll became a Lincoln log, covered with chocolate frosting, roughened to resemble bark.

Washington's birthday was another special occasion. Sometimes we listened to, or took part in classroom debates as to who was the greater president—Washington or Lincoln. We revered the Father of Our Country, but we truly loved Lincoln. He was of the "people." We retold the story of George and his little hatchet, cut out pictures of Washington crossing the Delaware, and learned pieces to speak at the program celebrating his birthday.

Both presidents' birthdays were events for programs, poetry reading, and patriotic speeches. But those weren't the only times we engaged in such activities. Friday afternoon "Literary Society" was a grand opportunity to show off our powers of memorization. We did a lot of memorizing in those days, and it is surprising how often I find myself quoting poems I learned back in the grades. Our reading books gave us quite a variety of poets and subjects, and our manner of recitation ran the gamut from stumbling hesitation to impassioned elocution. Declamatory contests were very popular, and debating teams covered many subjects and much territory.

Then it was time to get ready for Valentine's Day, and we worked hours fashioning home-made valentines. We cut red construction paper hearts in various sizes to hang on "baby-ribbon" and printed on them such thoughts as: "If of me you cease to think, my heart would SHRINK, and Shrink, and s-h-r-i-n-k!" When we saved up enough pennies, we would go down to the store on Cedar Street where you could buy fancy, fold-up valentines for a dime, stand-up ones for a nickel, and brightly decorated hearts for a penny.

The older kids sometimes spent as much as 75 cents on huge lacy or expanding ones for special sweethearts. Here, too, you could get penny candy—red cinnamon hearts, candy hearts with messages written on them, and heart-shaped paraffin "gum" filled with red syrup. Sometimes we caught glimpses of the comic valentines that were like huge colored newspaper sheets. These made cruel gibes at old maids, homely teachers, or dumb kids, and were not openly sent.

If you had a chance to help create the valentine box at school, you were particularly privileged and worked to make it a thing of art. The day the box was opened was a special one; sometimes you were even allowed to wear your Sunday dress and hair ribbons to school. Usually, too, there was a committee who provided a treat—cookies, cakes, or candy. And if YOU were chosen to pass out the valentines, you were in seventh heaven.

At home, we were thrilled to help Mama with the holiday baking. We cut out heart-shaped cookies, sprinkled them with red sugar, or frosted them and decorated them with red hearts. And how proud we were to carry our efforts to school for others to enjoy. Other days we watched as Mama prepared a cherry pie in honor of the Father of Our Country. We were either terribly nosy kids or Mama had a flair for dramatizing cooking; we seemed forever to be hanging over the table watching her bake. She'd sift a pile of flour directly onto the breadboard, add a good pinch of salt and a chunk of home-rendered lard, then work it in till she had pieces the size of peas. Then, judiciously, she added the water till the mixture blended and molded itself into a ball. With deft motions, she rolled it out to fit the pan, poured in the drained cherries, sugar, and flour to thicken, and fitted over it all a top crust with her own individual markings for steam vents.

Oh, the fragrance when it came from the oven, and the luscious flavor of fruit and flaky crust when dessert was served!

The days were getting a little longer and folks said that once you got the plants and sick folks through February, they always improved. The houseplants had to be moved away from the windows on the coldest nights so they didn't freeze, and about this time of year, the Chinese laundry man who did Papa's starched white shirts would give him a bulb which, put into water, would eventually develop into a gorgeous Chinese lily.

Leap year day brought parties at church or school—"socials" they were called. We weren't invited to those till we got older. There was much talk of women proposing, and games were devised to put the ladies in the forefront.

Weather is a great leveler, and February is a great month for weather. No matter who you are, you're still at the mercy of those howling winds and the pelting snow. Our activities during a blizzard depend upon where we are when the blizzard hits, and what our immediate needs are. To some it means the effort of getting back home to family; to others, worry and concern for those out in the storm, or whether fuel and power will hold out, or if telephone calls will go through. We compare stories of other

117

blizzards we've heard of or experienced, and we go about the business of waiting it out.

Memories of blizzards I've experienced are indelible. During grade school and high school days whether or not children attempted to go to school was left to the judgment of the parents. No radio bulletin informed us of road conditions. When I was in the lower grades we didn't have a telephone to let us know whether or not Papa got over the bridge to work safely. If the storm was bad when we got up, we didn't go to school. By the next day, the horse-drawn wooden plow would have cleared the sidewalks, and we were happy to get out after being confined to the house. Those who lived farther out — as did the Knutson girls, and the Pinneys — didn't usually get to school for a couple of days after a storm, although sometimes one or two of them would stay overnight at our house, or with other friends, if the blizzard hit while we were in school. (Martha Pinney must have believed that we lived on Johnny cake, because Mama always got the urge to bake it when it stormed.) We four girls loved having overnight guests. It always meant special privileges — and help with the dishes.

In March of 1924, there was a blizzard I will long remember. I was going to Milwaukee Normal, and our class was doing practice teaching in various schools in Milwaukee and the surrounding counties. But the blizzard changed everyone's plans; no street cars or trains were running and there was no way to get to your assigned school. Several days later, after partial service had been restored, I tried to reach Washington School, where I was to practice teach, but got only as far as Wanderer's Rest Cemetery. The conductor on the street car told me I couldn't possibly get through, so I had to go back to my cousin Myrt Stoneman's, where I boarded. On Monday I made another attempt. This time I walked up Lisbon Road, and a kindly older couple gave me a ride in a cutter through drifts that reached almost as high as the telephone lines. Both that year and the next, when I taught professionally at the school where I had done my practice teaching, the drifts were mountainous, and the storms seemed continuous.

I remember blizzards, too, out at Carlsville and Sunny Point Schools, but in those days I boarded close to the schools, and getting back and forth wasn't the hardship for me that it was for the pupils. They were taken to and from school by covered bobsled in winter weather.

Today we read of oil and gas shortages, of whole cities crippled from the effects of weather. Frozen water pipes, lowered thermostat settings, the feeling of isolation from having to stay out of the storms and sub-zero weather make us edgy. It's awful. But do you remember the winter of '36?

The February 7, 1936, *Door County Advocate* reports: "As if more than two weeks' cold wave were not enough, the weatherman brought on one of the heaviest blizzards since 1929 this past Monday and Tuesday. Wednesday's low was 27 below." I remember! Six weeks of sub-zero weather, mostly 27 to 29 degrees below. That was a winter. Too cold to let the children go outside, even for a ride around the yard on the sled. Too cold to do anything but stoke fires and exist as best we could. Those were Depression years, and life was not easy.

Still, we were lucky. We were living in the farmhouse on the orchard place that was the old homestead. In the fall, the house had been well banked with straw all around the foundation, and as winter drew on Stanley and I moved everything essential into two rooms—the big kitchen and the living-dining room, which was transformed into a triple bedroom. Ruth was four and a half, and Mary a fifteen-month toddler. And in those days of massive unemployment we were fortunate because Stanley had a job at Teweles elevator company.

We did our cooking on an old black range, and a space heater, whose pipe stretched across the room to the same chimney where the range vented, helped keep wintry blasts from penetrating too far inside. An old base heater kept the bedroom comfortable.

Blankets and weatherstripping further aided in sealing in what warmth we could muster. The three beds were piled high with wool comforters, and sometimes, when blizzards raged, we took hot water bottles or well-wrapped heated sad irons to warm our feet in bed. Other rooms—hallway, entry, pantry, and our "summertime bedrooms"—were shut off.

At first it seemed more or less an adventure. I kept thinking of pioneer days and of the stories I'd heard of the storms out in Nebraska and the Dakotas. But the novelty wore off as more of the same greeted us every morning, and our routine settled down to keeping fires going, keeping clean, and keeping fed.

Before leaving for work, early each morning, Stanley brought in extra pails of water, extra scuttles of coal, and saw that the wood box was heaped high. Then, taking his lunch pail, he plowed through drifts down to the road where the Model T waited.

A while later, Grandpa drove out from town, parked by the highway, and hiked up the hill to feed the cow, chickens, and all the cats and kittens who came running. They watched while he milked the cow, certain that their share of the milk was coming.

He would bring the milk into the house to be strained, and would pour a big crockery bowl full for us. The rest he took home in a pail. After he fixed hot mash for the animals, he checked the fires for me and opened the trap door that led to the cellar. Then he carried down the warm milk and brought up a cool bowl and any stored vegetables or canned fruits I needed, plus a bowl of apples for eating and cooking. I kept a hand on each of the girls so they wouldn't fall down the steps.

Then it was coffee-klatch time. I didn't make fabulous coffee; Aunt Olive was the one in the family noted for that. But Grandpa wasn't critical, and we enjoyed the leisure time while he warmed up and we caught up on news from town.

The old rocker by the kitchen window came into play now. Both girls climbed on Grandpa's lap, and he'd rock them and always sang: "Rea, rea, runkin. Hesta hestaprunkin—" They loved it. We were lucky to have such a wonderful grandpa.

Cooking plenty of stick-to-the-ribs food took a good share of the day. We had compressed yeast by then, so, when we made bread, we didn't have to sponge it and let it rise overnight. We'd never heard of frozen T.V. dinners (or of T.V., for that matter), but we had our own version of frozen food close to hand. All I needed to do was wrap up warm and duck into the closed-off pantry—a handy walk-in freezer—and choose cuts of beef or pork stored there. Not much variety, but a lot of good eating. The kettle sang on the old range all day, and the heat from the fires warmed the room adequately, except for those mopboards, fringed with a coat of ice all winter.

To scrub the floor was to transform it into a skating rink, so instead it got a quick mopping with hot water, then a rubdown with an old dry bath towel. There was a cistern pump at the end of the galvanized sink, but the water in the cistern (under the pantry) froze, and we had to keep the reservoir filled with melted snow or water from the pump outside. The icy water chapped our hands, but we rubbed vaseline or glycerine and rose water on them, and they soon healed.

Bathing facilities consisted of a tin washbasin in the sink and a washtub in front of the fire. Of course we had to walk to the little house out behind the granary. There we had a beautiful view of the frozen countryside, not to mention the arctic breezes coming up through the three-holer. Naturally the little girls couldn't be expected to be exposed to the elements like that, so a receptacle was provided for them inside the house. From today's point of view, all this might seem a hardship, but think of the advantages we had. With no water piped into the house, we had no frozen water pipes to contend with.

Nylon and other man-made fibers had not yet come into use, but we had good warm woolen clothing—sweaters and flannel petticoats, and khaki wool overalls (with triple thicknesses of material on knees and seat). The girls even had long underwear that I made out of the sleeves of men's old union suits. Warm coats and snow pants, made on my trusty treadle sewing machine from grown-ups' outworn coats, waited all those weeks for a good airing.

The time passed and we did have entertainment. The Atwater Kent radio was our pride and joy. It provided us with news of the outside world, music, recipes, mystery stories (the Shadow knows!), spiritual guidance, and comics like Ed Wynn, Jack Benny, Amos and Andy, and George Burns and Gracie Allen.

Kate Smith's singing brought joy; and I tried not to miss Mary Margaret McBride's chatter and recipes. I didn't follow the stories on "John's Other Wife" or "Ma Perkins," but I was a little sneaky about their premium offers. I discovered that these offers were made at the end of the programs, so I'd tune in then and jot down the free offer—flower seeds in return for an Oxydol box top or a package of cactus seeds from Twenty Mule Team Borax.

The girls had cut-out dolls—Princess Elizabeth and Princess Margaret, Shirley Temple, and the Dionne Quints. Paper scraps littered the floor and "pick-up time" was more like sweep-up time. The button box was a source of creative stimulation, often providing miniature building blocks for stages to act out paper-doll stories. While my sewing machine hummed, the girls made doll clothes and doll blankets.

While the windows were thick with frost, the girls would climb up on the day bed, scratch a peephole in the icy-patterned surface, and gaze out at a winter wonderland they couldn't visit. The windowsills held my collection of geraniums, begonias, and impatiens, while at the kitchen windows tiny seedlings, protected from the frosty pane by layers of newspaper, gave out a promise of spring. The steam from the ever-singing kettle spread humidity to the flowers and plants, while luscious food aromas and wood smoke mingled together.

Finally it seemed that the back of the winter was broken. There came a day when we could all go out to spend a half hour in the snow. We looked down the hill toward the highway, saw cars going by, and knew that soon we could go down to Goettleman Warner's again for Saturday night groceries and candy treats. So lucky we were! Fuel enough to keep us warm and home-raised food to keep us healthy. February, the fun month, was over.

March

March is such a capricious month that we have a love-hate relationship with it. Back in my grade-school days, March was ornery: the sun higher in the sky, now melting, and here and there a crocus peeping out. Then, suddenly, blustery winds and snow squalls. It was a little early for kites, hopscotch, and jump ropes, but some of the boys were sure to show up with their bags of marbles, and a corner by the school steps often sheltered a group of girls playing jacks.

Our overshoes had sprung leaks by this time, so when we waded through roadside puddles left by the melting snow, our shoes got wet. At night we'd have to stuff them with newspaper and put them on the stove mat to dry out.

As we made our way to school through the slush on the sidewalks, we listened for the trickle of water running under the ice alongside the road, and the sound brought an assurance of spring. The maple trees in our back yard showed signs of dripping sap, which we touched with our fingers and then licked, relishing the sweet taste. We would have liked to gather sap as our cousins in the country did, but Mama explained how many gallons of sap had to be boiled down to make one pint of maple syrup. Papa bought a gallon jug of the syrup every spring. Mama used to tell us what fun they'd had at sugaring off parties when she was young, and we envied her those good times.

Back in the "old days" (my sister Marian's kids once asked her if she'd come west in a covered wagon—I guess it all depends on your point of view, as to age), we'd gauge the weather by the spirals of smoke coming up from the neighbors' chimneys. Before we sat down to breakfast, we'd peer through the window cleared of frost and report, "Smoke's coming straight up from Reynold's and Scofield's chimneys; it's going to be a nice day." Then we'd sit down to our bowls of oatmeal or Cream of Wheat, bacon, boiled eggs in little egg cups, and oven toast. No radio or TV to provide news or music, but the teakettle sang on the old range, and we vied with each other to tell news we'd heard at school the day before. When Papa left to walk across the bridge to the branch bank, we got our hair braided, washed up breakfast dishes, and ran up into the cold bedrooms to make our beds before we left for school. Always in March we looked to see the first robin.

We had a saying that there would likely be a blizzard around St. Patrick's Day, and sure enough, it usually came. Winter had its last fling. Sometimes the storm was severe enough to keep us from school, and we used our holiday to make scrapbooks or to write letters. We bundled up and did the chores, like carrying in extra scuttles of coal, pails of water, and kindling and wood for the range, so Papa wouldn't have to do it when he got home. We used hard coal in our base burner, and we loved to watch the hay-colored flame behind the isinglass window.

In the evening, we watched Papa coming home in his heavy black overcoat, sealskin cap, and knit scarf covering nose and mouth. It was a long, hard struggle, coming home after dark, over the old bridge and the uphill blocks from town. He always said, "It's good to be home, I'll tell you. The storm flags are flying tonight."

After the blizzard, we would wake to a world of beauty and sometimes destruction, where the fury of the storm had torn down trees, broken huge branches, and piled drifts as high as the upstairs windows of the house. The tree limbs, fence posts, and window ledges wore a frosting of white; the remnants of our snowman had been draped in new garb. Since there were only two or three cars in town (automobiles we called them then) and those were set up on blocks in the barns or woodsheds that served as garages, we didn't have to shovel driveways. But we all turned to and dug paths to the road.

There was something about a late-winter blizzard that stimulated the palate, and the cook. When the old black range was going full force, the kitchen was cozy, and the smells and tastes made us forget it was freezing and blustery outside. It was soup weather, and we loved most any kind of soup. When we heard about Campbell's alphabet soup we begged Mama to get some, but she made chicken soup with rice, and told us to notice how rice cooked in soup forms its own alphabet.

When Mama wanted to make beef broth, we were sent to the butcher for a marrow bone and a piece of boiling beef. The rich broth simmered on the range all morning, sending out a tantalizing fragrance. Then, late in the afternoon when the broth was cooled, Mama skimmed off the fat and added barley, vegetables, and seasonings. This was one of our favorites, as was pea soup with chunks of ham and rice. But March wasn't all for eating and cooking. March also was a month when you had to look out for colds, and it was a good thing to be forewarned.

Papa should have been a doctor for he had a cure for nearly every ailment — most of them homemade. The fat from our Christmas goose was rendered down to make a base for camphorated oil. Mutton tallow was rubbed on our chests when we had persistent coughs. There were flax-seed poultices for boils, and bread and milk poultices for drawing out an infection. And I will never forget the pungent onion poultices that held heat so long they seemed almost to cook you.

Did you ever have to chew senna leaves when you needed to be kept "regular?" We did, and we hated them! If we were ill enough to call a doctor (and that had to be pretty serious!), most likely he would prescribe mutton broth instead of solid food. Dr. Kreitzer always did. I hated the mutton broth, too; when it cooled even a little it tasted of wool to me.

Ash Wednesday usually came in March, and this signalled the start of Mama's making hot cross buns every Wednesday. They were made much like her spice bread, with lots of currants, and they gave out a wonderful spicy smell while baking. She would cut a cross on the top of each bun when she shaped them, then fill the baked cross with powdered sugar frosting. Nowadays, when I make hot cross buns, I draw a line of sugar frosting across the tops of the baked buns in one direction, turn the pan and zip on another line — the crosses are made all at once.

We always paid special attention to St. Patrick's Day because there was Irish in our ancestry. Usually we had corned beef and cabbage for supper that night, with "red flannel" hash to follow next day. We made it a point to wear something green to school — a green bow at our collar or a kelly green hair ribbon. Sometimes there were box socials at school or church, or a card party at the local hall. The magazines of the day printed special menus and games and patterns for decorations suitable for the "luck of the Irish." Mama always sang "When Irish Eyes Are Smiling" and "Wearing of the Green." There was even one memorable celebration when we watched Papa do a bit of an Irish jig!

One St. Patrick's Day party during the Depression I remember well. It was before our daughter Mary was born, and Stanley had given me money for a maternity dress. Lane Bryant, which specialized in maternity clothes, had been in business for a short while, so I sent there for a dress. I was happy that it came in time for the party that the Priscillas of our church were giving. The dress was a green printed rayon in the Mother Hubbard style as were all of "those" dresses then. It was made with ties for expansion. I was very happy about the dress, until one woman who was also pregnant told me, "You know, I was going to send for a dress from Lane Bryant until I saw yours. I'm going to make myself one, but not that wraparound style." Well, so much for being humbled! In my Mother's day she wouldn't even have appeared in public when she was "that way."

One of my childhood memories is that our house was not as drafty and cold in March as it had been in February, so we were allowed to wash our hair every two weeks, but we had to stay in front of the coal stove, rubbing until the hair was dry. You rinsed your hair with lemon juice if you were blond, or, if your hair was dark, you used vinegar in the rinse. Then, after it dried, you braided it down to the end, to make it wavy, or if you wanted Mary Pickford curls, you put it up in rags. Mama said her mother would put her hair up on curlers made of tea lead, the heavy foil that tea came packed in.

I had a long bob with a hair ribbon fastened on top till I was eight or so. Then it was braided half way down, and a rubber band and hair ribbon were tied there. Later I wore the braids in cradles, with ribbons on each side. Wearing long braids to school could be a hazard. At the upper corner of each desk there was a hole into which a small glass ink well fit. We used steel pen points fastened into wooden penholders—no fountain pens allowed. The ink well was perfectly placed for dipping the ends of girls' braids.

A gift of new hair ribbons was something to cherish. Washburn's grocery store carried quite an assortment. When we were given the wide "water-silk" or bordered kind, we saved them for special days or programs at school. By the time we got to high school, the girls were wearing puffs at each side of their heads. You either snarled (teased, they say today) your hair underneath and then rolled it up, or you stuffed a "rat" made of combings inside.

Almost everyone had a hair-receiver on her dresser, in which you saved the combings, and I remember Mama once had a switch made of her combings. I can't recall her ever wearing it, though. Her dark brown wavy hair was heavy, so she didn't need the switch to form a big bun at the back. Some women wore their braids in a coronet; some twisted theirs into a knot. Some wore kid curlers (usually covered with a dust cap) to relieve straight hair. The first curling irons were heated in the chimney of the oil lamp. Later there were electric irons, water wave combs and clips, and, when beauty parlors blossomed, the torturous permanent wave machines, or marcel irons. When Irene Castle cut her hair, she liberated the women whose heavy "crowning glory" had for years given them continual headaches. But it took quite a few years before bobbed hair wasn't considered "fast." Those were the days when boys wore pompadours or the slicked back patent-leather look.

Of course we were still wearing our long winter underwear in March; Papa said we couldn't change to summer underwear until Decoration Day, and he claimed it didn't really get summer here till the Fourth of July. Our stockings looked pretty lumpy from folding over the surplus. The legs were fairly tight when we put on clean suits on Sunday, after our Saturday night bath, but each day they stretched more till, by Friday or Saturday, they were as wrinkled as an elephant's skin.

By mid-March Mama had a good start on her spring housecleaning. We knew that on Saturdays we had to help beat the rugs with the old wire carpet beater and lug things in and out for airing. The smell of ammonia, boiled linseed oil, and vinegar pervaded the house. Some years Mr. Stroh and his men would come to paper or paint the walls. Papa usually varnished the woodwork and the floor around the rugs, and Mama washed walls and did the curtain stretching. We hated house cleaning; the whole house was torn up for a couple of weeks. But we considered it a necessary evil.

Generally, the rhubarb, dandelion greens, or asparagus that we relished so in spring weren't ready, but we could hurry things along by preparing for Easter, with its promise of renewal. Winter was waning. The poet told us that the roots of the deep red roses would keep alive in the snow. We could even spot a few crocuses defying the weather. We thought of the tulip and daffodil bulbs we'd dug deep into the ground last fall and, in our mind's eye, pictured that colorful bed in bloom.

Spring would come. Roller skates would come off their hooks. Baseball bats would come out of the closets. We never had to go the sulphur and molasses route to cure spring fever. Maybe Papa didn't see the value of that concoction, or maybe we had enough natural vim and vigor to make it unnecessary. Everywhere around us there were evidences of the coming of spring. Capricious March couldn't last forever.

April

Way back when I was growing up, we made a big thing of April Fool's Day. Jokes ranged from the "Oh, look at that robin out in the yard" type to more elaborate ones played by ardent practical jokers. Often, however, Mother Nature did the fooling, bringing a snowfall reminiscent of winter. But the crocuses and daffodils usually survived, the ice in the bay started breaking up, lilacs and box elders were in bud, birds built nests, and there were yards to rake and trash to burn. When the trees and lawns start putting on new dress the urge to shop for new clothes tempts us. Or, at least it did when we were young. Sturgeon Bay, in the early 1900's, still had a few wooden sidewalks; there were livery stables where garages would be later on. Third Avenue was Cedar Street then, and the blacksmiths were busy: Mr. Alex Johnson in his shop across from the old Washburn feed store; Mr. Richard Maples; and Mr. Pease on the Sawyer side. Sometimes we'd peep in to watch them at work at the forges.

When we were in grade school, spring meant a little longer to play after school and still get home well before dark. Some days we might have permission to go home with a friend to jump rope or play jacks at her house until time to run errands. Saturdays we took little adventure trips into the country, where farmers were out on the land and all kinds of spring signs were to be seen.

We had little rituals that seemed to go with spring—like "stamping robins." We'd raise a fist to our mouths, then stamp twice on our open left palm for each robin we saw. I guess the object was to see who could count 100 robins first. We "stamped" white horses, too.

Another sure sign of spring was seeing Old Joe Marden walking down Lawrence Avenue on his way from Shivering Sands to town for supplies. He carried a sack over his shoulder, and his long hair was always tied with colorful ribbons. We gave him a wide berth, not from fear, but because the story went that he fried his potatoes in skunk oil!

But looming above everything else that the coming of spring brought was spring housecleaning.

Remember the curtain stretchers out on almost every front porch? And the heavy poles propped up to support the parlor carpet while we took turns banging and beating it free of winter's dust with the old handy-dandy carpet beater?

Most folks were in a flurry to have the housecleaning finished by Easter; walls washed, windows gleaming, out-buildings whitewashed, some rooms calcimined or redone by the paperhangar. Women in dust caps and long gingham aprons gave an ammonia shine to windows, pictures, and mirrors. Gardens were spaded as soon as the soil was right. And on Good Friday, we were sure to plant garden peas and sweet peas.

Coming home from school we might be asked to help carry in the just-washed bedspreads, mattress pads, and comforter covers from the line — the sickly-sweet smell of yellow soap and steam still permeating the kitchen. We ironed the bleached flour sacks and sugar sacks so they could be made into dish towels, garter waists, or underskirts, running the old sad irons over a cake of beeswax so they would glide over the material. It was a good way for girls to learn to iron; starched things and linen tablecloths would come later.

We also were taught the proper way to do dishes: the yellow soap at hand for the suds and an extra dishpan for the rinse water, glasses first, then silver, dishes, pans. No Chore Girls or steel wool pads; fingernails were made for scraping stuck-on food from the pans. We used every excuse possible to get Mama to allow us to soak the kettles till the next meal (providing, of course, that it wouldn't then be our turn to wash them). The enameled kettles would chip easily, so we had to take extra care in scraping them.

In Home Ec. class (we called it Domestic Science) we were taught to use a wood-handled knife to scrape pumice from a brick and then to use this for scouring. We didn't have dish "cloths"—they were dish rags; and in summer we threw the soapy dishwater out on the garden to help kill bugs on the plants. We had soft water from the cistern for washing; pump water was heated to boiling for the rinse. Our cistern was up over the kitchen, but some folks still had rain barrels.

Soda (Mama always called it saleratus) had lots of uses besides as a leavening agent. Picture cards of various American birds were included in the soda box, and we treasured our collections. We watched Mama sharpen her knife on the edge of a stone jar or crock, and when we got old enough it was our chore to wash and shine the kerosene lamp chimneys and trim the wicks so the lamps would burn evenly and not smudge.

All those jobs didn't do much for our fingernails, but then no one had heard of nail polish. Nail files came into use, and we trimmed our nails with fingernail scissors, cleaned under the nails and pushed down the cuticle with orangewood sticks, then buffed them to a shine with a chamois-covered buffer.

One sure sign of spring was the dandelions that appeared everywhere and that we were sent to dig out. Most grown-ups liked the tonic effect of dandelion greens in salads. We'd hold a blossom under a friend's chin to "see if you like butter," and when the stems of the flowers were long enough we'd make dandelion chains and weave crowns of the blossoms to wear in our hair as make-believe queens. We must have been very much impressed with the Astors and the Vanderbilts, for we pretended that's who we were when we dressed up in long clothes and dandelion crowns.

Often in April we would interrupt our play to pull green onions or hunt for asparagus — "sparrow grass" some folks called it. Rhubarb, too, would be showing its red stems; the first rhubarb pie was quite a treat.

April brought the anniversary of Paul Revere's ride, and we memorized at least part of the famous "Midnight Ride" poem, which we recited along with other "memory gems" at our Friday afternoon Literary Society in school.

If we were having an early spring, we might get permission to walk out to the woods to hunt for arbutus, that elusive, fragrant, delicate pink-and-white blossom that hides under the dead leaves, its long runners trailing like strawberry plants. We gathered the lovely cup-shaped blossoms very carefully, being sure not to pull up the roots, and carried home a treasured bouquet to Mama. We looked for wintergreen berries, too, knowing of special spots where they grew.

While the house was being refurbished and our slim wardrobes brightened with buttons and bows, we sort of roughed it, with only blankets on the beds and shades at the windows till the comforter covers were tied back on to their wool batts and the curtains came off the stretchers with scallopy points where the pins had held them tight.

We'd have quickie meals of raw-fried potatoes, hamburger patties, creamed cabbage and cottage pudding with raspberry sauce; or ham and eggs, riced potatoes, and canned peas, with raisin rice custard for dessert.

We liked housecleaning meals; there were never as many dishes to do afterward. The new crop of maple syrup had come, and we loved that on baking powder biscuits.

Eventually the house was ready and our clothes were ready, and all that was needed was the spiritual readiness that Easter brought to our hearts.

The year I turned 16, I looked forward to Easter with more than ordinary eagerness. I had been promised a new spring hat. Usually I just inherited one of the older girls' hats and rejuvenated it with a new ribbon, a bunch of artificial violets or daisies, a beaded buckle, and most likely a color transformation with Colorite dye. The dye came in various shades in a dauber-topped bottle, like shoe polish. I can still smell its pungent banana oil odor and feel the crisp stiffness it imparted to a tired old straw hat.

Two millinery shops in Sturgeon Bay displayed beautiful creations: flower- or feather-trimmed, with gauzy veils and wide or narrow brims. Each time Mama sent me downtown on errands, I lingered at the windows. I might not look like a fashion plate, but for once, at least, I dreamed of looking like a well-dressed young lady. No more of that kid stuff, with streamers hanging down the back of my hat, or elastic fastened under my chin! I made up my mind and changed it 50 times before the time came to go shopping.

When the day finally did arrive, Mama went with me to choose the hat. I was thrilled beyond words. I had saved a dollar and a half toward the purchase from my baby-sitting jobs where I earned 25 cents for an evening. Papa said he would make up the rest.

I decided on a hat of a fine black straw. It was perfect—simple, yet rich. Its only trimming was a wide black grosgrain ribbon, with a flat bow in front. The wide brim reached from sides to front only, a bit like a Quaker bonnet. "It's a pretty hat, " Papa said when he saw it, "but it looks as if a cow chewed a piece out of the back."

Even this left-handed compliment didn't dash my spirits. I pressed the old rose tweed coat that Vera had passed on to me, wiped my patent leather slippers with Vaseline, and each night I added a little prayer to my usual "Now I lay me down to sleep," asking that the weather wouldn't be inappropriate for spring hats, coats, or shoes.

The Saturday before Easter—Holy Saturday—was busy, a busy day for everyone. The fragrant smell of caramel rolls and hot brown bread, and the tangy smokiness of the Easter ham boiling on the back of the range filled the air. Mama's lemon-jell cake, our traditional Easter dessert, stood tall and beautiful. We all helped to decorate it, shaping marshmallows into bunny rabbits with long paper ears and dots of chocolate for eyes, mouth, and whiskers; covering the top with coconut, sprinkled with green sugar to represent grass; and placing tiny jelly beans in nests in the grass. There would also be Mama's delectable lemon meringue pie for dessert, or maybe feather-light "dandy pudding" made from Mrs. Groenfeldt's recipe. We cooked potatoes in their jackets for Sunday night's potato salad, made with our favorite old-time boiled dressing, and we boiled a couple dozen eggs for dyeing later in the evening. Some of them would end up as deviled eggs on the supper table.

With lunch over, kitchen floor scrubbed again, upstairs and downstairs cleaning and dusting finished, we were free to make our own personal preparations.

I had a special dream. The ads in *Ladies' Home Journal* and *Woman's Home Companion* had been describing a miraculous beauty aid, a Woodbury soap facial. It was applied like a mud pack and sounded so simple. First, though, I washed my hair, using Mama's home-made shampoo, a jelly-like substance made of 5 cents worth of Ivory soap and 5 cents worth of salts of tartar dissolved in three quarts of hot rain water. It made your hair soft and silky. I toweled my hair dry, then I filed my nails and buffed them to a light shine. My sisters had rituals of their own to prepare themselves for the Easter parade.

When the bathroom was free, I gathered my paraphernalia together and set out to make myself beautiful for my new hat. The Woodbury soap had been expensive—all of 20 cents—so I followed directions carefully, first washing my face, working up a thick lather and smearing it all over my face and neck, and letting it stay on for 10 minutes. I looked as if I were wearing a green iron mask; I couldn't talk without cracks appearing in all directions. The girls laughed and teased — told me it would never come off, that I'd have to go through life with a crinkle-crepe skin and slits for eyes, nose, and mouth. Privately a bit scared, I shook my head vigorously in defense: I was willing to suffer to be beautiful.

When the 10 minutes were up, I rinsed off the mask, though I did have to rub rather hard to get off all that lather. Our cistern had run dry of rain water, so Mama told us to pour a few drops of benzoin in the well water to soften it. This gave the water a milky look and a pleasing odor.

I fussed and struggled, carrying the teakettle of hot water back and forth between basin and coal range, because our faucets gave only cold water. Alternately, I steamed my face with hot washcloths, then applied cold cloths, and finally I began to feel the sensation of glowing skin as described in the magazine ads.

But as I patted my face dry I was aware of an unusual burning and smarting. Looking into the mirror I was horrified to see that my face was fiery red, with overtones of purple! I hadn't realized what the treatment could do to my sensitive skin. I tried patting it with ice water and bathing it with witch hazel, but it stayed that angry red. I was almost hysterical. How would that face look under the brim of my new hat tomorrow? Nothing that Mama or the now sympathetic girls said could console me.

To make matters worse, I had to exchange a book at the library, and I just knew everyone I met would think me a freak. "Wear your new hat," Mama told me. "That wide brim will hide the irritation; no one will notice." I didn't believe it, but it did give some measure of protection. I strapped on my roller skates and skimmed downtown, looking neither right nor left. At the library I hurriedly chose another book and brought it to the desk. Miss Lown, the librarian, gazed at me. "You're not coming down with something, are you, Grace?" she asked. "Your face is so flushed." I mumbled something about getting chapped in the wind and fled before I disgraced myself with tears.

All through the evening, as we helped dye Easter eggs and then laid out our clothes in readiness for the early sunrise service, I was despondent. Our four Easter baskets were brought down from the upstairs closet, and we divided the colored eggs and arranged them carefully. We knew that Mama would put one of her luscious chocolate-covered fondant eggs in the center of each basket before she "hid" them in their usual spots; behind the piano, the big chair, the leather-covered mission davenport, and— Marian's—in plain sight, under the center table.

When Mama called us at five the next morning, I jumped up and peered in the mirror. The inflamed look had disappeared and just two bright spots remained on my cheekbones. I sighed with relief, dressed in warm clothes— our new finery was for the later service—, and Mama and we four girls walked to church. As the sun was rising, we were singing "He is rising." Later we walked to church again, for the regular service. This time Papa was along. As he looked approvingly at his four girls dressed in their Easter

best, he smiled at me and said, "You look mighty pretty, young lady."
I felt a special glow, not brought on by the facial.

The church was jammed. The colorful array of hats and wraps vied with the display of lilies on the altar. The choir sang a beautiful anthem. Hallelujahs rang out loud and clear. And in my Easter bonnet I was aware of ethereal beauty—the blessed assurance of life everlasting; the Risen Christ!

May

When I was a little girl, May was the prime time to dig dandelions for spring salads. The April crop was small by comparison. We ate the greens, usually fixed with a hot bacon and vinegar dressing, as sort of a spring tonic, because we'd had few if any greens all winter. Sometimes we would get watercress from Big Creek, and, of course, there was rhubarb, but by and large we were limited to root vegetables and cabbage all winter.

The dandelion flowers' sunny faces made many a bouquet for children to carry with grubby little hands to mother. Sugar bowls and jelly glasses on windowsills held the offerings, and not even an orchid could be more appreciated.

When the dandelions went to seed, we'd pick the fluffy little balls, blow hard to make the winged seeds fly off, and count the remaining bits of fluff to "tell what time my mother wants me." If you blew hard enough to release all the seeds, that meant you could stay out to play a long time. Farm women stripped goose feathers in the spring to make the thick, soft downy pillows that were every housewife's pride. Wool was carded and made into batts, to be used for filling in next winter's warm comforters.

The nice thing about memories is that they don't spoil, no matter how long you keep them. Certainly the memories of old times and old friends remain unspoiled for me. I remember making May Day baskets of construction paper in Miss Minor's third grade. We filled them with wild flowers and hung them on a door knob at home to surprise our mothers. Years later, when I lived with my own family in Iowa, our children hung cornucopia-shaped baskets on our neighbors' doors on May Day evening, then hid and watched the gift received. Often they were rewarded with a candy bar for their efforts. They thought it better than Halloween.

Martha Pinney Tallman, a high school friend of my sister Vera, called on us not long ago. It was so enjoyable to reminisce with her, particularly remembering the time Vera invited me to the Maypole dances at Lawrence College back in 1920. It seems like yesterday. Mr. and Mrs. George Washburn gave me a ride to Appleton, as their daughter Genevieve was studying music at Lawrence. It was the first time I'd been that far away from home. I had often read about Maypole dances, but seeing one gave me something to talk about for months afterwards. Furthermore, we had stopped to eat at a restaurant on our way home — one of my very few childhood experiences of eating out.

If the May weather turned warm, Papa might permit us to leave off our long winter underwear. Even so, we still had our cotton undershirts, pantywaists, outing bloomers, camisoles or "shimmy" shirts, and ruffled petticoats to protect us from cool spring breezes. And that was the time of year when we would beg to wear heavy sweaters instead of winter coats to school.

On May evenings we were sometimes allowed to play out after supper, since there was usually yard work to do after school and, if it were an early spring, some gardening. Planting the garden was a happy, cooperative family effort. Early in May we girls would be told to sort out and sprout the potatoes in the cellar and to set aside the seed potatoes. We weren't particularly happy about spending a Saturday morning down there instead of enjoying the spring sun, but when Papa came home that evening we all turned to, helped cut the potatoes with the eyes, and then dropped them into the holes we had dug along a string stretched between two sticks. Peas had been planted earlier, while it was still cold; now we planted radish, leaf lettuce, pepper cress (Papa's favorite), carrot seed, and set onions.

During World War I, when Congress decided that daylight saving would be a good idea for farmers and for those raising "Victory" gardens, we had an extra hour to hoe and pull weeds, and to collect potato bugs in tin cans with a little kerosene in the bottom. We counted the bugs very carefully because we got two cents for every hundred. This money we stashed away to be spent at the big Fourth of July celebration in Vendome Park.

We were fascinated with weather vanes, for Papa was always concerned with the direction from which the wind blew, no doubt because of his years on sailing vessels. We used to recite "When the wind against the sun dost run, trust it not, for back it will come." The wind had a lot to do with the way the fish would bite, with the way you hung clothes on the line, and with flying kites.

The rainbow also held fascination for us, and we speculated on the pot

136

of gold at the end. We had our own rainbow-maker in our dining room, a hanging lamp that had a painted shade. Hung all along the metal edge were prisms, which we used to detach and hang in the window so we could watch the rainbow colors that spread to every corner of the room. There were rainbow colors in the woods, too: the lavendar of hepaticas, the blue of violets and bluebells, the green of the jack-in the-pulpit, the yellow of buttercups and cowslips, the orange of touch-me-not and Indian paint brush, the pink of spring beauties and wild roses, and the red of honey-suckle.

May was also a great month for making mud pies. Vera and I had a table and oven made of old planks and located out by the woodshed, and we concocted all sorts of muddy goodies. Often, at the north side of the shed, we found little drifts of snow, which we used for frosting on our pies and cakes. Near the woodshed door there grew a patch of Sweet Mary. I wish I could raise a patch of it today. Mama used to sing a little ditty about mud pies. I imagine she taught it to her primary pupils, when she was teaching out in Nausawaupee in her younger days. Years later I asked her to write it out for me: "Tell me little ladies, playing in the sun. How many hours till the baking's done? Harry builds the oven, Lilly rolls the crust. Susie buys the flour, all of golden dust. Pat them here, and pat them there. What a dainty size. Ring the bell for dinner. Hot mud pies."

In 1914, President Wilson proclaimed the second Sunday in May the official Mother's Day. Recognition of the day was largely the work of a woman named Anna Jarvis, but as far back as 1887, Mary Sasseen, a teacher in Henderson, Kentucky, had her pupils putting on programs honoring mothers. Even before that, in 1872, Julia Ward Howe, the "Battle Hymn of the Republic" lady, had suggested setting aside a day to honor all mothers. When Anna Jarvis finally succeeded in her efforts, she designated a pink carnation to be worn in honor of living mothers, and a white carnation in memory of mothers who had passed away. At first, Mother's Day was not an occasion for gift giving; later the day became commercialized and presents and cards were considered a matter of course.

I remember sitting in church one Mother's Day with a very small wig-glebug daughter who was not at all interested in what was being said from the pulpit. Straining to keep her from disturbing surrounding pew members, I suddenly heard the preacher say, "Like mother, like daughter," and I remembered my own restless spirit and inattentiveness as a child. So many wonderful Mother's Days, and a few martyred and sad ones, have come and gone. I am thankful that Mama left me a heritage of cherished memories.

It was about the middle of May, the year I was a senior in high school, that four of us Camp Fire Girls decided to earn special merit by going on a 20-mile hike. Jessie Poehler, Frances Cheeseman, Elsie Wiegand, and I started out early one Saturday. We packed our lunches and caught the Ahnapee and Western train that took us all the way to Algoma. That in itself was an adventure for me. My only previous train ride was once when Mama had taken us over to Sawyer, and we had walked back. The morning of our adventure was sunny and a little cool. We wore middy blouses and plaid wool skirts, heavy knit skating sweaters, and cowhide boots. We must have worn tam-o-shanters, too, for Mama would never let me go that far bareheaded.

When the conductor called out "Algoma!" we got off the train and walked around the town a bit, stopping for ice-cream cones. Then we started on the road back to Sturgeon Bay. Just outside Algoma, we found wild flowers growing by the wayside, a little later than at home, because of the nearness of Lake Michigan. We sang as we walked, joked, and found a nice picnic spot where we ate our bag lunches, then continued on. A short distance farther, as we were passing a farmhouse near the highway, two big rams came down the sloping bank and headed for us.

Elsie and Frances made a great leap across the ditch on the other side of the road, then crawled under the barbed-wire fence, where they were safe from the creatures' reach. Jessie and I weren't so quick. Grabbing sticks to protect ourselves, we discovered that if we faced the animals they just followed us warily. But as soon as we turned our backs, their heads went down, ready to butt us.

My heart was in my throat; it's hard to say "Go 'way!" when your tongue is stuck to the roof of your mouth. And it wasn't easy to walk the next quarter of a mile backward, knowing those rams were out to get us. The other two girls worked their way along the inside of the fence opposite, until we came in sight of the next farm, where a woman came out of the house and toward us, carrying a long stick. She spoke in stern tones to the sheep. "Go on! Get you home! Go on!" Meekly, they turned around and went in the other direction. "They do it all the time," the lady told us. "Come and sit on the porch awhile." She brought us cookies and cold milk, and we were soon refreshed enough to go on.

It was nearly six o'clock when we got to the old wooden bridge, where we suppressed a desire to try walking the railroad trestle. We knew what would happen to us if someone told our parents.

What a wonderful welcome-home aroma greeted me as I opened the back door. Saturday night baked beans, boiled ham, hot rolls, and devil's food cake. I was starved. But first I had to answer to Papa. "Where have you been, getting home this late?" (Banking hours, those days, didn't include Saturday afternoons.) I explained about the hike.

"Well, of all the crazy fool things to do! Taking the train to Algoma and walking back! Well, young lady, if you're not old enough to know any better than that, you can just forget about getting a watch for graduation." I washed up for supper but wasn't at all worried about the wristwatch. I knew that he and Mama must have been discussing my graduation present, or the threat wouldn't have come to his mind so readily. Besides, he was too softhearted to deprive me of what we then considered the epitome of graduation gifts. I sat down and enjoyed my meal.

May usually was a rainy month, giving occasion for all sorts of weather predicting. We said, "Rain before seven, clear before eleven." If everything on the supper table was eaten, we'd predict a nice day tomorrow. If we saw chickens or birds oiling their feathers during a rain, we were sure it would keep on raining for quite some time.

The year that Marian was born, on May 17th, the cherry trees all bloomed early. Most years it was closer to Decoration Day before we were surrounded by orchards white with bloom. We reveled in the beauty, and in the fact that school would soon be out. On Marian's second birthday, as we were singing "Happy Birthday" to her and telling her to blow out the candles, she bent a little too close to the cake, and suddenly her red-gold curls were ablaze, and she was screaming in fear and pain. Luckily, someone had the presence of mind to smother the flames with a napkin, but Marian's forehead had a burned spot that took a while to heal. We were all too shaken to enjoy the cake.

Toward the last of May, we had what was called "field day" at school. All the schools in the county met in Sturgeon Bay for track meets and other competitive athletic events. In the afternoon, after we had eaten our picnic lunches, there was always a spelling bee. What an honor for the school whose student won! Sometimes field day was combined with Arbor Day, where we took part in planting a tree on the school lawn.

So many May memories revolve around Memorial Day. Shortly after the turn of the century, when the observance was held on the 30th, it was a very big day indeed. The entire community took part; it was a day to decorate the graves of loved ones and, especially, to honor the men who had died for their country. It was a big day for the veterans of past wars. And for dwindling numbers of Civil War veterans, members of the Grand Army of the Republic — the "boys in blue" — this was the most important day of the year.

The last surviving member of the G.A.R, in our area was Henry J. Grandy, or Grandpa Grandy, as we all called him. He was the father-in-law of William Maples, who operated the Halstead-Maples Hardware Stores for many years. We lived across the street from Maples', on Poplar Street, so Grandpa Grandy, with his snow-white hair and long white beard, was a fascinating member of our neighborhood. We often slipped over to sit on his front porch and listened to him tell stories of the "good old days," and of Civil War days in particular.

On Memorial Day he was an honored participant and rode in the parade in full dress uniform. Before the advent of cars, I imagine he rode a horse in the parade, as he had served in the cavalry. In his late years, he rode in an open car and took an active part in the ceremonies.

Grandpa Grandy was born in October, 1838, in Clinton County, New York. He was 23 when he enlisted in the Fourth Illinois Cavalry Regiment, at Earlville, Illinois, in 1861, and became a member of the advance guard of General Grant's army, called the Army of Tennessee. Once, while Grandy was riding into battle, a shot from a cannon killed his horse, wounded another soldier, and killed an orderly. But Grandy was unhurt. After the war, he farmed at Institute. Then, around 1900, he moved to Sturgeon Bay, where he lived with his daughter and son-in-law.

Perhaps the reason we were so happy about parades in those days was because we were always in them. After school on the day before Memorial Day, children went picking wild flowers to decorate the graves next day. Purple and yellow violets, anemones, mayflowers, spring beauties, trilliums, and bloodroot were the usual varieties we found. We placed them in water overnight, then carefully wrapped the stems in damp cloths and tied them in paper for carrying.

We all gathered at the school for the march to Bayside Cemetery with our flags and our flowers. It seems that love of country, and of its flag, were taught us along with the ABC's. "Three cheers for the red, white, and blue" was not just a meaningless phrase. We were told: Red means "be brave," white means "be pure," and blue means "be true."

No one apologized for flag-waving. Prominent citizens spoke at the program in the cemetery; the flag was lowered to half-staff and recognition was given to all the old soldiers present. Then the school children placed their wild flower bouquets and flags on the veterans' graves. After the program, many families had their first picnic lunch of the season, complete with lemonade carried in two-quart Mason jars and drunk from tin cups.

Grandpa Grandy, our link with history, died on January 6, 1923, as active in peace as he had been in war. General MacArthur said, "Old soldiers never die; they just fade away." But Grandpa Grandy, the last of the "boys in blue," has not faded from memory. Many of us are proud to be Americans and unashamed to show our love of flag and country, because we were influenced by men like him.

June

All of a sudden, it's June, and the world is alive with aromas. Shortly after the sun has come up, there is a special fragrance outdoors that brings you closer to nature. You notice first the freshness of the air as you saunter about breathing deeply.

From the orchard the odor of apple blossoms greets you, delicate perfume with a suggestion of spice. You walk over toward the trees and cut a branch to enjoy at closer range. The dew is still on the grass, and as you move through it, the moist, earthy odor rises to greet you. You stoop to pick a dandelion—tangy scent with a slight vinegary suggestion. The sprinkles of white strawberry blossoms growing wild on the side hill appeal to you; bees are hustling in and out of their little cups. You become aware of the powdery feel and smell of pollen.

A puff-ball bobs against your leg; you pull it from its stem and open it to find a dry smoky film issue forth; it reminds you of a dusty vacuum cleaner bag. You walk on. Under the trees is a fair-sized patch of asparagus. Reach down and gather some, nipping the stems just below the soil level; notice the rank smell of soil, the piquant odor of the vegetable.

The apple branch in your hand, you turn and walk along the dusty path toward the flower beds. Tulips are in bloom; there is no noticeable odor there, just a suggestion of sachet. Dwarf iris send out a mellow sweetness. The short border of chives throws off its onion flavor, subtle and aromatic.

Stand a moment in the dew-drenched grass and breathe in deeply. All of the odors you have encountered are permeating the air. You find it impossible to analyze any one: together they combine to smell like a June morning.

June is the month when activities crowd in on us all at once—weddings, showers, graduations, gardening, vacations, summer sports, and barbeques. But when I was growing up, family barbeques were unheard of. Sometimes we'd cook wieners, or toast marshmallows over an open fire, but no one had an outdoor grill, at least, not until about the '30's. Then, it was likely to be an outdoor fireplace in the back yard. Picnics usually started about Memorial Day, and there would be strawberry socials, ice-cream socials, Sunday School picnics, and shortcakes as often as possible. Shortcake! How we looked forward to that! Mama's shortcake was the baking powder biscuit kind, feather-light, and heaped with berries, and cream over the top.

I always thought Mama's's shortcake couldn't be surpassed, that is, until I was married, and heard from Stanley how *they* had shortcake at his home. And when I saw and tasted my mother-in-law's shortcake I agreed it was super. Hers was biscuit dough, too, but made in the large cake pan, split into layers, buttered, and piled with berries on the first layer. This was covered with a second layer turned cut-side up so the juice would soak in, then topped with more berries and whipped cream. Carried in on a huge blue platter, it was a sight to behold—and a pure joy to eat. Once, when I entertained some friends out on the farm, Grandpa brought me a case of the huge berries from his patch on Strawberry Lane, and Grandma helped me serve shortcake to the group—our own strawberry social.

By late June, my sisters and I used to go out to Larkin's to pick berries. We picked every other day, usually from 7 A.M. until noon, having finished our lunches of leaf-lettuce-and-radish sandwiches by 10 o'clock. We were allowed to wear overalls for this job because we crawled along between the straw-filled rows. We also wore bandanas, to keep from getting sunburned. We took the rows in turn, one on each side, but we were happiest when we got to pick on the "fertilizer" rows, as they had the biggest berries. Berries were usually ripe by the end of June, close to the Fourth of July, and then there was a spell before the cherries were ripe. Once in awhile, if it was very hot, we were permitted to go in swimming. Our modest bathing suits covered us well.

Mama always ordered a crate or two of berries, and it was a family project to sit out on the porch and hull them for canning or eating. No Certo then; the berries were cooked down, with an equal amount of sugar, and tested for jelling in a saucer. We always hung around for tastes, and loved to watch the jeweled-colored jam being poured into glasses, then covered with melted paraffin. Mama canned some berries for sauce, too, and in our family we liked the sauce on our French toast. During the season, we had cherry dishes at least two meals a day, usually eating them sugared, with thick, yellow pour-cream. We hadn't heard of cholesterol then and didn't worry about the richness.

One June while we were growing up, Mama thought it would be nice to raise bees. Papa had a sweet tooth and always enjoyed honey. So, she got a hive, and learned how to handle the bees when they swarmed and how to get them into another hive. I remember the old jingles we would repeat "A swarm of bees in May is worth a load of hay. A swarm of bees in June is worth a silver spoon. A swarm of bees in July is not worth a fly."

When the bees swarmed, it was up to Mama—dressed in veiled hat, gloves, sleeves, and overall legs tied close—to quiet them by using a bellows-like gadget that smoked. But somehow, it seemed that usually when the bees swarmed, Mama was at church. Verna would then don the beekeeper's garb, follow the swarm to a tree, or wherever they flew, find the queen bee, and get her and the rest into the new hive. We stood watching at a safe distance, wishing we were brave enough to do that.

June was a time to lie on the grass and watch the clouds sail by. We used to see swarms of "Green Bay flies" everywhere—store windows plastered with them, streets and sidewalks so covered they'd crunch under automobile tires or people's feet. I guess they really were mayflies. For two or three weeks every summer you'd see folks collecting them for fish bait. About this time, too, mosquitoes had made their unwelcome appearance and spiders dropped down on us unawares. We always said they were bringing a message.

During the summer months we spent a good share of our mornings in the kitchen watching or helping Mama and taking turns with upstairs or downstairs chores. One of the things that always fascinated me was Mama's terms of measurement. When she was giving a "receipt," she'd say a "pinch" of this, or a "smidge" of that; call for a scant or a heaping tablespoon, or for butter the size of an egg, or a couple of shakes of flour or salt to taste, and perhaps a quart of flour. Baking might be done in an "afternoon" oven—one that had been allowed to cool down after the heat used to prepare the noon meal. Cakes were tested with a broomstraw or toothpick, and I used to watch Mama take a pan of yeast biscuits from the oven, separate a row, and test with her finger to see if the dough would spring back when she touched it. Then she'd dip a small piece of cloth in sugar water and brush it over the rolls for a lovely glazed top. Squeaking was a test, too. Bread should turn out well if the dough squeaked when you kneaded it.

We were always eager to tell Mama about the things we learned in Home Ec. Most housewives made cream sauce or cream gravy by mixing a little flour with water, stirring that into milk, and adding a chunk of butter about the size of a walnut. At school we were taught to cook the butter and flour together, then add the milk, and stir till smooth. We were taught the proper way to level off a spoon or cup of flour, and how to be exact in measurements. Everything was made from scratch in those days, so meals had to be started early.

When the garden was ready we might have peas, beans, or lettuce every day, but the fresh vegetables tasted so good, we didn't mind having them over and over. No one had freezers to handle the surplus, and canning vegetables at home wasn't advised until about the '30's, when pressure cookers were introduced. A favorite dish made with green beans was what Mama called slumgullion: beans, new potatoes, and little onions cooked with a chunk of ham.

We didn't know anything about vitamins—hadn't even heard of them—but somehow we seemed to get them in our diet. We were open to new methods of food preparation as they came along. Our families discussed the merits of creamery or dairy butter. We bought bananas by the dozen, not the pound. Hamburgers were unknown to us, but meat balls were a favorite. I was so fond of them that Mama once said she'd get extra meat so I could eat all I wanted. It was almost a year before I could eat meat balls again.

I remember a June birthday party I attended when I was eight or nine, all dressed up in my checked linen dress, white stockings, and patent leather slippers. We had homemade ice cream and what was to be a patriotic birthday cake. That turned out to be a red, white and green. I heard the women discussing it, saying the egg yolk must have turned the blue sugar coloring green. But it was a delicious, fluffy cake anyway, piled high with frosting and nine pink candles on top. When I tried to say what a good time I was having at the party, it seemed as if the other girls always interrupted. Finally, I got so disgusted, I said, "Mama, make them stop butting out." How they laughed at me! But I can recall debating whether "butt in" or "butt out" was correct.

Mama's's forget-me-nots and ferns grew thick around the north side of the house, where I'd sit on the outside basement steps and ponder why I so often said the wrong things. Mama didn't allow any fighting and she always told us, "Never let the sun go down on a quarrel." One day when I'd been over at Genevieve Jacob's all afternoon she wanted me to stay for supper. I was in a spunky mood and said, "You never come and stay with me," after which I flounced out of the house and down the street toward home. But I was facing into the sunset and Mama's rule haunted me. So, I turned back, and apologized. How they all laughed at me then, too.

June of 1922 was very special for me; it was the year I graduated from high school. The commencement exercises were unusual, because ours was the first class to wear caps and gowns. We felt so proud and grown up, marching across the stage to receive our diplomas. Palmer Johnson wrote the lyrics to our class song, which we sang to the tune of "Believe Me if All Those Endearing Young Charms":

We stand at the gate of a vast new world,
Our faces are turned to the light.
Through the four years of our high school life,
We have striven to work for the right."

When the class chose "We Serve" as a motto, I remember demurring with the flip remark, "Sounds like a hotel or restaurant." Little did I know that 28 years later that motto was to become our family's way of earning a living, when we built the restaurant!

When vacation time came, in my young years, although we had more time to play, we still had our chores to do. I remember, in particular, those associated with washing and ironing clothes. We each took our turn at ironing towels, sheets, and underwear that wasn't starched. Starching involved a different process. Papa wore white shirts with separate collars, and Mama used cold-starch and ironed the collars dry and stiff, from the soaking-wet stage. Shirt fronts got the cold-starch treatment, too. Tablecloths, petticoats, and gingham and percale dresses were dipped in a solution made with those little bumpy chunks of Argo starch that had been stirred into cold water paste. Then boiling water was added and the solution cooked at the back of the range till it made a smooth liquid. Mama often added a piece of that blue bar of Satina so the iron wouldn't stick and the starched white ruffles kept a whiter look. For best results, the clothing had to be well sprinkled, wrapped, and allowed to stand for several hours to "mellow." We learned the trick of getting into ruffles, ironing sleeves first, and always being careful to test the iron with a wet finger so we wouldn't scorch the clothes. Once in a great while, if we ran out of Argo, Mama would substitute with starch made from cooking rice, but that starch was not as crisp. We had an extra ironing board — without legs but well padded with old sheets — that we stretched between two chairs, so one of us could iron starched things while someone else ironed the plain laundry. Gingham and embroidered dresses for us girls, shirts for Papa, and dressing sacques and long percale dresses for Mama and Grandma were hung over a clothes rack till dry enough to be put away in the closets. If clothes needed patching, this was done before the garment was washed, and the patch was almost invisible when ironed. Skillful mending and darning was a matter of pride. You learned to weave the thread with exactness and to darn socks so that they wouldn't hurt the foot. Families kept darning balls and glove menders — something like little egg-shaped lollipops for getting into glove fingers — and passed them on from generation to generation.

The intensifying heat of the June sun once tempted Mama to try sun bathing, as she had seen many young folks do. The impulse came over her one day as she was taking clothes off the line. Carefully, she spread out a large bath towel from the clothes basket and lay down on it, her hand shielding her eyes from the sun. The sun felt good, and she felt drowsy. Then, suddenly Mrs. Florence Nebel's voice startled her. "Mrs. Keith, are you all right? Did you fall?" Embarrassed, and a trifle miffed, she scrambled up, limber as a youngster. "No, I was just getting a little sun." So much for sunbaths.

Nowadays, June is the month for Father's Day. The holiday hadn't been established when I was in school, so Papa didn't get any special notice on that day. But he was always special to us. He was quiet and serious, with an unexpected spot of humor, and the precepts he taught us were the rules he lived by: security in the love of family, honesty at all times, friendliness to everyone. "You can always be nice to people," he said. He never promised us anything for doing a chore, but I can still hear him say, "Well, now, I think a little girl deserves something for doing such a good job on that lawn." I loved to listen to the stories he made up about "Mamie-go-wan, in the North Woods." But best of all, he was a "friend," and we were proud to call him Papa.

July

Somewhere around the Fourth of July, in the days before the first World War, the early cherries were ripe, or at least, ripe enough to pick "on the stem." Most of the pickings were sent via train in sixteen-quart cases to the cities. All of us neighbor children helped pick in nearby orchards. Willis and Harriet Johnson, and Annie, Esther and Lucile, from the Olaf Johnson family, joined us in Mr. Hutto's orchard, right next to our house on Poplar Street. The Minor boys, of course, worked out at their father's orchard near the cove. We moved on to other orchards when Mr. Hutto's was picked. No experts, we — in fact, I never succeeded in becoming a fast picker. But it was a way of earning money for the County Fair to come in August, and for school supplies and clothes. When the factory began canning cherries we picked "off the stem," pails tied around our waists.

The younger children, and sometimes the mamas who came after their wash was on the line or when the bread was out of the oven, were allowed to "cream" the bottom branches. We kids were cautioned to set the ladders on level ground, and not to climb in the trees. When the mothers came into the orchards they brought lunch and, usually, jars of lemonade. Each morning, when we started picking, we would eat the juiciest and ripest cherries, but after an hour or so our tongues felt a little sore, and we settled down to more picking and less eating. Some orchard owners had a reputation for being extra strict, making you pick up all the cherries that fell on the ground, and chastising those nervy kids who dared have cherry or cherry-pit fights, or who broke branches.

Out on the highway, a girls' camp called Boyce's provided pickers for some of the large orchards, and when those girls would string across the road on the way to town for an evening at the movie, we called them "cherry snappers." Cherry snappers were what we called the cedar waxwings, too, and they really did snatch the ripe cherries — although the Bordeaux mixture used as a spray discouraged them somewhat. Some of the older girls got the chance to work in the cherry factory, where they earned more than the pickers. They could usually save enough money to go camping down at Nicolet Bay. What fun! At the fairgrounds there was a Boy Scout camp that provided pickers. My husband Stanley said what he remembered most about the camp was the peanut-butter sandwiches they got for lunch. (He also long remembered the delicious potato soup he had at Gordon camp.)

We had a cherry pitter at our house, a disc outfit that ran the cherries through into one bowl and spit out the pits into another. We were always willing to turn the handle of the pitter, and it meant we'd be rewarded with Mama's flaky cherry pies, or a sample of the little test dish of jelly made from the juice.

Mama often told us about the first cherry pie she made after she was married. She and Papa had company, Great-aunt Effie and Uncle Nate, so she wanted the pie to be special. The crust was tender, browned to just the right degree, with exactly the right amount of sugar added. But, though she had been used to doing a lot of the baking at home, she forgot one thing—to pit the cherries. The company got quite a surprise when they bit into the pie.

The cherry pitter came in handy, too, when making other favorites, especially cobbler and canned cherries that we stored in Mason jars and brought up for sauce or pie during the winter. We loved the steamed cherry puddings, too, with thickened cherry juice for sauce, and Mama's cottage pudding or cornstarch pudding with cherry sauce to top it.

The Fourth of July, of course, was the highlight of the summer. There were often speeches and a band concert at Vendome park, and we'd go as a family, proudly dressed in our Sunday best, white embroidered dresses with wide ribbon sashes and matching hair bows. We always wanted to celebrate with firecrackers, but Papa was disapproving. "Why, you could blow your fingers right off, or lose an eye. Those things are dangerous."

"But couldn't we just have some of the tiny firecrackers? They won't hurt us. Some of the big boys even have some giant firecrackers."

"Well," Papa said, "if someone else jumps in the lake, is it any sign that you have to?"

Pleading got us nowhere. We were allowed to have sparklers, though, to wave from the front porch like fireflies. And we could see, high in the black sky that night, the sky rockets some of the privileged kids were allowed to set off.

More than anything else, the Fourth of July was a day for picnics. I remember a picnic of long ago, when disappointment turned into a happy experience. I was probably about seven that summer, and we had long planned a ride to Clark's Lake, with a picnic dinner.

That summer we had a boarder, Mrs. Mamie Jones, a widowed friend of the family. She earned her livelihood by taking orders for the *White House Cook Book*, an esteemed book with recipes from all the presidents' wives, descriptions of state dinners, and correct table settings. Mrs. Jones was very personable; we admired her appearance, too, for she never went out on her calls without a hat and gloves, and usually a parasol, too. We girls loved to hear her talk about her travels. She was a wonderful story teller and read so beautifully that we sat enthralled. She wrote many of her own favorite recipes in Mama's Sturgeon Bay cookbook.

For this particular Fourth, Mama had been especially busy with food preparations all the day before. We were up early, and all hands turned to in packing the food to take along. Papa walked down to the livery stable and came home in a surrey (I don't remember if it had fringe on top,) pulled by a beautiful horse — glossy black and high spirited. We looked forward to a pleasurable ride. Papa, Mama, and the baby rode in the front seat; Mrs. Jones sat in the back with Vera, Verna, and me. The food was packed at our feet, covered with an old bedspread to help keep it cool and free of dust. We sat proudly on the seat, waving at our friends and savoring the prospect of a day in the country. Papa said "Gid-yap," and the horse clip-clopped on his way.

But not for long. We had just turned the corner, when the horse went lame. Papa got out, examined the horse's shoes, and said, "Well, this horse can't take us to Clark's Lake. And he was the last horse in the livery stable, too." Three little girls set up a wail, but Papa was adamant. No traveling with a lame horse. He turned horse and surrey around and stopped at the house to unload all our paraphernalia, leaving us frustrated and unhappy. Mama went in the house to put on her apron. It looked as if it was going to be just an ordinary day, after all.

But Mrs. Jones had other ideas. She soon had us carrying jars and bowls of food, while she spread the checkered tablecloth on the lawn, in the shade of the maple trees. Remember, this was 1911 B.B. (before barbeque), and you never saw a family eating out in the yard — picnics were for country, parks, lakes, or the fairgrounds. But this was fun! Papa walked back from the livery stable, and we all sat down on the ground and surveyed the spread.

Potato salad, made with boiled salad dressing; deviled eggs; sliced boiled picnic ham; cabbage, shredded thin and dressed with vinegar, sugar, and bacon bits. Two-quart Mason jars filled with lemonade with pieces of rind bobbing around in it, to enhance the flavor. Homemade bread with butter and thin slices of pressed chicken loaf. Radishes, onions, and lettuce from the garden.

But the last and best was the freezer of homemade ice cream, the cannister packed in a nest of chopped bay-ice and coarse salt, while the flavor mellowed. We made our ice cream from rich egg custard, cooked till it coated the spoon, then cooled and blended with beaten egg whites, whipped cream, and plenty of vanilla. We served it smothered with juicy strawberries. A thing to dream on! We would happily turn the crank on the freezer till our arms ached, all the time anticipating that frosty treat.

After our meal we were so full, we rolled on the grass, and lay on our backs to watch the cloud pictures in the sky. What a day! I can hear Mama asking Mrs. Jones, "Weren't you disappointed?"

"No," she answered, "I've had so many disappointments in my life, just missing a buggy ride wasn't hard. There was still dinner. And we were all well and safe and sound."

Between the picking of the Early Richmond cherries and the Montmorencies, there was plenty of opportunity to sit on the front porch. Evenings always brought the grown-ups there, watching while the neighborhood children played "Hide and Seek," "Auntie, Auntie-Over," or "Pum-Pum-Pullaway."

The mosquitoes usually were bad, but the ladies brought out their fans, which did double duty brushing away the insects and moderating the heat. Merchants often gave away cardboard fans with colored pictures of roses, pansies, or Gibson girls, and advertisements that boasted the merits of their shops. Some read: "With best wishes for your good health — use Dr. Dennis' Catarrh Remedy." Or, "Brown's Bitters; the best tonic." And, of course, some had pictures of Mrs. Langtry, "the Jersey Lily."

Palm leaf fans were popular, too, as were Japanese fans, some of them silk-screened with lovely oriental pictures and teak handles. Lacking these, we folded paper in pleats and waved it, or simply used a fold of newspaper, which was handy, too, for swatting the pesky bugs.

Porches were often screened in, or had mosquito netting tacked on. The L-shaped side of our porch had trellises, covered with Virginia creeper, which provided privacy when we slept out to escape the heat of the upstairs bedrooms. The front porch was a good place to gather when we had a rainy day; it was also a cool spot where we hulled berries, pitted cherries, shelled peas, or snapped beans. Grandma and Mama rocked in their rockers and Papa read the *Door County Advocate* and *Modern Woodman*. When neighbors stopped by to visit, Mama would bring out a pitcher of lemonade, made with cold water freshly pumped. We had no ice except that cut from the bay in winter, and Papa wouldn't let us use it in food or drink. Watermelons, though, were cooled in a tub of water with a big chunk of ice.

Patching and darning were useful things to do while sitting on the front porch. (No self-respecting housewife would dream of sitting and reading in the daytime.) Mama gathered the basket of socks and darning cottons in her apron, and, putting on her thimble, set to work weaving in the jagged spaces of worn heels or toes. Grandma did beautiful patching, making patches that matched the weave of the cloth and became almost invisible. But if we got pesky playing near her chair, her patience was short, and we were apt to get a rap with her thimble to remind us to stay clear.

Grandma wore aprons that were the long gingham kind, tied at the waist. That's the kind Mama wore, too, in the kitchen, and it came in handy, when she was going outside, to shoo the flies away from the screen. She would lift the corners of the hem and fill her apron with kindling, vegetables from the garden, or windfalls from the trees. It was useful, too, for gathering eggs and for bringing in clothes from the line when a sudden shower came up. Those gingham aprons were also used to lift hot dishes and pans from the oven. Eventually, they turned up as dish towels after they had served their primary purpose. Mama had "good" aprons to put on in the afternoon, or to whisk on when unexpected company showed up. And she had fancy ones that she wore when helping serve at Ladies Aid or W.C.T.U. meetings.

Sewing carpet rags was another thing to do while sitting on the front porch, as was stitching patch work quilts. Occasionally Mama would entertain a few ladies during the day. Then they'd sit rocking and visiting, while Mama made the egg-coffee, set out the lunch, and called them inside to eat. We knew some people who played cards on their screened porch, but since our card games were limited to Flinch and Old Maid, we didn't take part.

Although we lived close to the Bay, we didn't do much swimming as girls. Papa never allowed us to go into the water unless he was along. We spent many hot afternoons in the shade, taking turns pumping cold water on our feet. We rubbed our fiery skin with cucumber peel, then smeared buttermilk on our arms and faces to help fade the freckles. And *nobody* wore shorts in those days.

Sometimes Papa would take his older girls down to the shipyard to watch a launching. And often Chief Frank Stroh would take his family and ours in his launch—Papa steering, and Mr. Stroh at the engine. We got to see Chambers Island and Guff Island as we traveled all the way up the Bay side of the peninsula. What fun! No far away adventures for us. The year I was eight, though, Mama and Papa took a vacation to Upper Michigan, and we three older girls were left in the care of Grandma. For two weeks we got away with a lot that we couldn't do while our folks were at home, like climbing on top of the woodshed, walking barefoot through puddles in the road, and going down to the library after supper. We brought out our best dolls and games to play on the front porch, and badgered Grandma into cooking our favorite dishes. She was very deaf, but good at lip reading. We had to watch our conversation at the dinner table, or she'd tell us, "That's no way for a young lady to talk."

Most years we got to spend a week or two on Uncle Sam's farm in Jacksonport. How much help we were in their busy season is a question, but we did do dishes, peel potatoes, and prepare vegetables. One chore we thoroughly enjoyed was grazing the cows down the "lane," often finding wild raspberries or blackberries at the wayside. Aunt Bertha used to send along a jar of raspberry vinegar, and I doubt if anything could be more refreshing.

We thought we were pretty smart to have an uncle who had a Shetland pony farm. We didn't have to go to the County Fair for pony rides. At the close of a hot working day in the fields, the whole family rode down to Lake Michigan in Uncle Sam's Model T, which he also used on his mail route. Although the lake water was cold and we were dressed in our overalls, we romped and paddled through waves or ripples and were rejuvenated.

July afternoons were wonderful for reading in the dappled shade of the maples, watching ant hills and caterpillars, and knocking potato bugs into a can of kerosene. And then the Chautauqua came to town. We felt privileged, in a day before radio or television, to be able to hear and see nationally famous concert artists, lecturers, and others. The great tent might have been stifling, but that didn't diminish the thrill we experienced one bit. We were Americans all, with equal opportunities and the right to be proud of it.

August

I was thinking, the other day, about going to the fair when I was young, and I remember fair time wasn't in August then, but rather the first week of September. There were ripe sheaves of grain, huge pumpkins and squash, beautiful rosy tomatoes, all for display in the agricultural building—garden produce that did the growers proud.

The women from the various churches served dinners on long wooden tables set up on saw-horses and placed under the protection of a big tent in case of rain. It seemed as if it often did rain during the fair. I guess that's why the time was changed to the last week in August, right after the state fair.

Not many of us got to the state fair, but our own Door County fair was a red letter day in our lives. How we saved our nickels for rides on the merry-go-round and for the pop-corn wagon and the ice-cream stands! On Children's Day we got there as early as possible, for there was no school that day, and we got in free. Sometimes one of the shooters at the shooting gallery booths would give us the kewpie doll he won.

The weather may have been hot in town, but we were always admonished to bring along a warm sweater and maybe rubbers and our "cravenettes" in case of rain.

Usually we visited the exhibits first. The display of baking was always tempting; we were eager to see who got the blue ribbons for the cakes, biscuits, cookies, and loaves of bread. And we had to see the animals. "Watch out! Don't get pecked by the hens or nipped by the geese. And don't drag your sweater on the ground; you're holding tight to your pocketbook, aren't you?"

Next came the educational building with its booths containing examples of studies from pupils in the different schools around the country—the one- and two-room country schools, and the grade and high school in town. On display were examples of perfect arithmetic, reading, penmanship, spelling, and history papers; examples of drawing; and "busy work," classic poems, laboriously copied. When we found our own work we were mighty proud.

On Friday, the women in the church tents served baked fish. Sometimes we were allowed to eat there or, if we didn't hike out to the fairgrounds till afternoon, Grandma fixed lunch for us at home. On Saturday afternoon, all the business places in town closed and everyone went to the fair. Papa rode out on his bicycle, and sometimes we girls got a ride in a neighbor's wagon. I remember Mama telling us that someone had asked her how she was going to get to the fair and she told him "shank's mare." It seemed such a funny expression to me instead of "walking."

Eventually we all gravitated toward the fence by the race track. Usually the kids didn't go in the grandstand. If Sir Allard, Mr. Alex Johnson's beautiful horse, was running, we were doubly excited because we were friends with the Johnsons. Papa loved the races, too, and we knew that when they were over, he'd treat us to another ride on the merry-go-round and to ice-cream cones.

But fair days weren't the only memorable August events. In my teen years, as a Camp Fire Girl, several of us earned a week at a Bay Shore cottage for picking a small plum orchard when the owner, Cedric Dreutzer, couldn't get any other pickers. Camping out at a cottage in those days was really exciting. We swam three times a day, hiked, and toasted marshmallows or wieners on the beach. We wore knickers, or gym bloomers, and middy blouses. If we were really daring, we rolled our stockings below our knees. One evening I got thoroughly frightened when I saw a big snake. I screamed as loud as I could and kept screaming while the poor snake slithered away. Soon a neighbor from a nearby cottage came over, carrying an ax. He thought someone must be attacking us, and had come to our rescue. To this day I'm ashamed of my cowardice.

If we girls went to our Uncle Sam and Aunt Bertha's farm at Jacksonport, Papa and Mama instructed us to help out as much as we could, but I don't know how much real help I was. We tried, though, doing dishes, preparing vegetables for dinner, and making beds. Cousin Lou laughed as she told me I wasn't in the city and didn't have to peel the potatoes paper thin. I told her the rhyme about the little girl whose mother hurt her feelings by making her peel the peelings. We sang old time songs while doing dishes.

Aunt Bertha had a lovely old pump organ, and on rainy days it was fun to sit with the practice book on the rack and play "Grasshopper Green" and other simple tunes, coached by finger numbering. The what-not in the corner of the parlor was intriguing, too, with so many knickknacks on those corner shelves. I remember commenting on the fact that people around Jacksonport spoke of visiting at "the Bay" when they went to town. Later that week we read in the *Door County Advocate* that we'd been visiting at "the Port."

Once when I went along with Uncle Sam to the other forty he owned, Babe, the Shetland pony I was riding, decided she didn't want me on her back. So she lay down and rolled in the dirt. I got off in time, but, determined to get the better of the pony, I remounted her to try it again. Well, Babe was as persistent as I was, and once again, down she went. I walked the rest of the way. At fair time, Uncle Sam brought the ponies up to the fairgrounds, where they gave rides to the children. Having an uncle who raised Shetland ponies seemed to me a feather in my cap—I could have rides for nothing!

Door County has always been known for its natural beauty, and when I was a little girl it had already become a popular summer resort area. One of the early resorts was "The Cove," operated by M. E. Lawrence. Its cottages were "furnished with all individual requirements except cooking utensils." Guests at the Cove took their meals at the dining hall, which was described as being "centrally located." The Cove boasted "a bathing beach large enough to accommodate a thousand bathers. Smooth, velvety, sand bottom, no stones, crabs, or reptiles." Good fishing and reasonable rates (seven to ten dollars per week) were other attractions, and a pleasure boat, the *Advertiser*, made regular runs between the city, the Cove, and the ship canal. The *Advertiser* also sailed between the city and Idlewild—"A fine place for picnic parties."

The Tourist Home at Idlewild was run by Tellif Haines. Their advertising told us that visitors were loud in their praise of the beautiful scenery and invigorating atmosphere surrounding the home. Scenery was "unexcelled;" wildflowers grew everywhere. Within walking distance was the famed Sherwood Point lighthouse, Lover's Leap, the high bluffs of the government reserve, and views of the beautiful islands in the harbor. Among the accommodations that the Tourist Home offered were still water bathing, fishing, a fine harbor for sailboats and rowboats, acres of grounds for all kinds of outdoor games, and a fine, smooth road to the city for automobiles, carriages, and bicycles. Their rates were $2.00 per day or $8 to $10 per week; single meals were fifty cents. The management "guaranteed everything to be kept in a neat and tidy condition, both in the buildings, and the surrounding grounds. The culinary department is in the charge of first class artists and the best of meals are served."

The folder advertising these and other resorts in the Sturgeon Bay area goes on to say that "Numerous summer cottages dot the eastern shore of the bay, where excellent fishing and bathing are afforded. Rural free delivery leaves the mail at their door each day, and the tourist is so situated that he can be constantly in touch with his business if necessary."

Transportation facilities at that time included the Ahnapee and Western Railroad; the Goodrich Transportation Company, whose boats made daily arrivals and departures for the two-day trip to and from Chicago; Green Bay Transportation, with boats that made daily trips between Green Bay, Menominee, and Upper Michigan ports; and the Hill and Hart Transportation Co. Local people also made use of these means of transportation. It was always a treat to go for Sunday dinner out to the Cove or Idlewild. For those who had the means of travel, a visit to the Thorpe Hotel at Fish Creek, the Eagle Inn or Anderson Hotel at Ephraim, or the many other well known tourist hotels in the northern part of the county, was a lovely way to entertain guests. There was chicken every Sunday and angel food cake that literally melted in your mouth. I recall one trip around the county in 1911, when Aunt Grace was visiting. Harry Dana drove us in Mr. Fetzer's Buick, and it was an all day trip, memorable because of ten flat tires and dinner at the Eagle Inn. At the Anderson Store, Verna and I each bought penny dolls, little china dolls, about two inches high, with movable arms.

For several summers, we rented Johnny Feurenstein's cottage at Clark's Lake for a week or two. What great fun, swimming, rowing, fishing, sailing with Papa and watching him as he trolled for muskie. Mama made bread, biscuits, French toast, and pancakes on the camp stove. She showed us how to find herbs, gold thread for a sore mouth, and sarsaparilla. And we hunted for beechnuts and hazelnuts. One day Ken Greaves took me across the lake to get some of the many little frogs one found there for bait. We were roundly scolded by Papa; I was never supposed to go in a boat unless he was along. Some nights we toasted marshmallows over a campfire and sang Papa's favorite hymns, always with a nautical flavor, because he had sailed in his young days. "Jesus Savior, Pilot Me," "Brightly Beams Our Father's Mercy," and "Let the Lower Lights Be Burning." The trees and the water seemed an appropriate setting for those songs.

There were families in the city who took tourists into their homes. I remember the Cheeseman place, by the fruit growers' dock. The senior and junior Mrs. Cheeseman were famous cooks, and Clarence Cheeseman, who worked in the grocery department at Washburn's, was a favorite of ours. When Lucille Johnson and I had a penny to spend, we'd hie ourselves down to Washburn's and wait till he could wait on us. Then we'd stand enthralled while he reached into the candy counter for a big handful of "little mixed" to put in a bag for us. We'd sit on the step of the feed store and count out the pieces—"One for you, one for me." Most of the time it came out even and the candy lasted a long time.

In August, after the cherry and raspberry picking, came apple time. Just about everyone, or his neighbor, had Transparent, or Duchess trees, and we kids had green apple tummy ache many times. But then the apple treats would appear on the table: apple dumplings, apple crisp, apple spice cake, apple sauce, apple kuchen, and, best of all, good old apple pie. We were glad to help peel the fruit for the treats they provided. Peaches appeared soon, too; we always got ours by the bushel. Peaches meant pie, cobbler, and sliced peaches in our Jello. We stood watching Mama dunk the wire basket of peaches into boiling water, then slip the skins off. Canning time was fun for us; such lovely spicy, savory smells, extra tastes, and always the anticipation of the canned sauce, jellies, jams, and relishes to be brought up from the cellar in winter.

Lots of homes, especially those in the country, had summer kitchens to prevent the intense kitchen heat from invading the rest of the house. No matter that the cook and her helpers sweltered while putting up canned stuff for winter—you could usually find a breeze to sit in while peeling, husking, or scrubbing the garden bounty, and you got a bit of a change running out for wood to feed the hungry maw of the old range. We got our recipes and techniques from Grandma, the neighbors, or the old Sturgeon Bay cookbook. There were women who never "gave out" a recipe, but Mama considered it a compliment to be asked for something she made especially well. Canning was a part of summer, and every self-respecting housewife was proud of her stock of home-canned foods.

In those days, table etiquette was drummed into us at every meal, and, because Papa thought that "Fletcherizing" was important to one's health, we four little girls sat at table, chewing each mouthful rhythmically, 30 times, to ensure good digestion. In the early '20's, Emily Post's book of etiquette came out, and much of our dining table conversation centered on that. I wasn't particularly confident about when to stand when an elder entered the room, but I knew which fork to use and how to refold my napkin before placing it in the napkin ring. When Papa was called to Chicago to attend the funeral of a relative, he reported that he hadn't felt like a hick because Emily Post had taught him to tilt the soup spoon away from him and sip from the side, not the end, of the spoon.

By the end of August we would be getting ready for school again. New hair ribbons, new gingham checked dresses, a new pencil box, and our patent leather "Mary-Janes" shined up with a bit of Vaseline. A bouquet and an apple to take to the teacher, and a trip down to Washburn's on the afternoon of the first day to buy our text books. The tourists and summer visitors had gone home, and everything was back to normal. Fun, family, friends, school routine. The golden thread of love woven through the years. I thank God for these memories.

September

Summer flies by, and September brings school days and school memories. New pencil box and tablet in one hand, a bunch of golden-glow blossoms and an apple for the teacher in the other, we'd make our way down to the building that in my day housed all eight grades and high school.

Almost always we had a brand new gingham dress and new hair ribbons for the first day of school, and often the seamstress, Miss Knudson or Miss Graf, had spent the week before getting our fall wardrobes ready. We enjoyed those creative sessions. Mama would shrink the material for our new dresses, then soak it in salt water for at least an hour to set the color. Mama also made our underwear — petticoats with lace flounces, garter waists, unbleached or flour-sack bloomers, and outing flannel bloomers for winter to wear over our long underwear.

In the lower grades I wore an apron over my dress to keep clean. My sisters, Vera and Verna, always managed to keep their dresses immaculate, but I was a "messy Bessie," my dress rumpled and my hair straggling out of the braids that Grandma had plaited. Grandma had a tight hand with hair, pulling it back till you thought your eyes would pop. But she could tie a lovely bow in your hair ribbon, and she softened the strain by telling stories about when she was a little girl.

We three older girls all had Miss Jenkins in the primary grades. She had been Papa's teacher at Egg Harbor so she was really an institution — a formidable one. When someone misbehaved, she was apt to send the person out to fetch a switch from one of the maple trees surrounding the building. If you thought you'd do best with one of the little ones, how wrong you were! Those little twiggy branches could sting like everything when she switched your legs, and you learned it didn't pay to whisper or giggle in her class.

We learned our ABC's by writing on slates, with slate pencils, and we had little wet rags for erasing. And I believe we used Heath primers. In class we had to memorize,

The goldenrod is yellow;
The corn is turning brown;
The trees in apple orchards
With fruit are bending down.

We would come home on that first day eager to report on the new teacher, whom we had already decided was going to be crabby or nice, the "awful" boys who teased us, or the new kids with their "new-fangled" clothes.

The best part about starting school again was being with all the friends who were in our grades last year. We lived in the third ward, and seldom got down to the first or second ward, unless we had permission to walk home after school with a friend who lived there.

It wasn't until high school that we had the opportunity to meet an entirely new group of students. Sawyer kids and Sturgeon Bay kids grew up almost as if they lived in foreign countries, and we hardly saw each other until the Sawyer graduates came across the bridge to high school in Sturgeon Bay. Eighth grade graduates from other parts of the county would come to Sturgeon Bay High School, too, if they had relatives to stay with or found a place to board. Some brought food and clean clothes with them each Sunday night, returning home Friday nights to family life and re-supplies. But the Sawyer young people made their trek over that long wooden toll bridge four times a day. Only if you lived far enough out, or if a storm threatened, were you allowed to bring your lunch and eat in the gym. At noon, the timing was close: 20 minutes to get home, 20 minutes to eat, and 20 minutes to get back to school.

School children weren't required to pay the five cent bridge toll during the day. But if you came across in the evening for literary society or to go to the library, or the movie, you did pay. In the winter, when there was no ship traffic, you could walk across the ice from the end of Maple Avenue over to the Hans Johnson boat works.

Mr. Losli was in the bridge's toll house, and another man was in charge of the turnstile to open the draw. When the Ahnapee and Western train came in over the railroad bridge, you had to be alert so that you wouldn't get caught on the trestle. Walking the railroad bridge was considered a scary and daring thing to do.

In high school we were seated in alphabetical order, girls on the left side, boys on the right. The assembly room was also study hall for free periods, with one of the teachers at the desk on the rostrum, to supervise. Behind the teacher were tables, chairs, and book shelves; this was the school library. Some daring individuals would try to get away with murder behind the teacher's back. In my day, Mr. "Sox" Soukup's rule was absolute. You could hear a pin drop when he spoke to the pupils about "bulldog tenacity."

During my last two years of school, Mr. Gotham was principal. He and his family moved into the Stanton Minor house, near us, and Ruth Gotham became a good friend of mine—a member of my "bunch."

Coming home from school at noon on those warm September days, the pattern seldom varied. On Mondays we'd arrive to a steamy kitchen, with the sickly-sweet smell of yellow soap bubbling from the old copper boiler on the range. If the boiler leaked, Mama pushed a glob of bread dough into the hole, like the Dutch boy at the dike. Luckily she almost always baked bread on Monday.

Usually a big pot of vegetable or chicken soup was simmering at the back of the stove. We'd eat heartily, and then one girl would turn and rub the socks in the washing, one turned the wringer while Mama rinsed the clothes from the boiler, and one carried out a pail of hot soap suds to scrub the outside bathroom facilities with an old broom.

On Tuesdays Mama would have the stove roaring to heat the sad irons, and we took over at the board to smooth out the dishtowels and handkerchiefs. Macaroni and cheese often showed up on Tuesdays, or hash, along with baked apples and oatmeal cookies. Then, as soon as the dishes were done, we were out the door and on our way back to school.

Those fall days were crammed with chores—peeling apples for pies, quartering and seeding apples for apple sauce, and pickling pears, peaches, and crabapples. Beet relish, beet pickles, corn relish, and "slippery Jim's" all were a source of pride to the housewife in a day when buying commercially canned products was considered slack and extravagant. In fact, some folks resorted to burying the empty tin vegetable cans in the yard in dead of night, so nosey neighbors wouldn't find out! But not everything was home made. Each fall the dray man brought big wooden boxes of soda crackers and sacks of prunes, raisins, rice, sugar, tapioca, split peas, yellow-eyed beans, flour, oatmeal, and cornmeal.

Fall housecleaning meant plenty for us to do. We lugged and pounded and scrubbed as fast as we were able, so we'd be free again for hikes or trips to the library. When you skated down town to buy round steak or dried beef for supper, the butcher would give you a piece of sausage to eat as he expertly rolled up the package with ends tucked securely inside, needing no string fastening.

One of our least-enjoyed chores was ironing. It was hard to keep the sad irons hot enough to iron embroidered ruffled petticoats dry and shiny. The blunted points of the irons wanted to catch and tear the open work. Dresses were a little more fun, once you got the knack of doing the sleeves. We weren't allowed to do Papa's shirts, but the linen tablecloths, sprinkled until they were almost soaking wet, had to be pressed over and over to bring out the woven pattern. Pillowcases rewarded your work with the three-dimensional look the embroidered flowers gave. Sheets and towels got quick licks unless Mama was nearby to inspect.

Now was the time we carried in the house plants that had been outside all summer. All the pots had to be washed off and some plants would be transplanted to the fernery.

September was the month, too, that the coal stove was moved from its summer corner to the place in the kitchen where it sent out the most heat. Papa would put up the stove pipe, which had been stored in the woodshed all summer, and the coal man would deliver a ton of Pocohantas (Peccky-hentas one old man used to call it).

Fall colds, as most other illnesses, were treated with home remedies. We caught la grippe and quinsy sore throat, not flu. Our "wonder" drugs were quinine or castor oil "to give you a good cleaning out." Some kids had to wear a smelly bag of assafetida around their necks. Goose grease, fortified with gum camphor, was the stand-by at our house, and we were lucky if we didn't have to endure flax seed or onion poultices to ward off pneumonia.

By and large we were well nourished and got the necessary vitamins because we ate things that were good for us. Our table didn't seem completely set until the cut glass vinegar cruet stood at Papa's place, handy to douse the usual Saturday night baked beans, or to pour on tomatoes or sliced cucumbers. Old Dr. Kreutzer warned us never to eat the peelings of the cukes, and to be sure to cut the ends off down to the seeds. He claimed to have known a girl back in Germany who died from eating cucumber ends! Naturally, you soaked the cucumber slices in salt water for an hour before fixing them for the table.

One of the things we liked about the fall was that all the ladies organizations started up again—Woman's Club, W.C.T.U., Missionary Society, and Ladies Aid. When Mama would entertain any of those groups, we were sure to hurry home after school, often bringing friends along to help us enjoy the sandwiches, cakes, cookies, or fancy desserts she had made.

Mama had a huge thresher-type coffee pot for those special occasions, and making coffee was a ritual. First she'd grind the beans in Grandma's coffee grinder, moisten the grounds with egg and add some of the shell to settle them, carefully measure the boiling water into the pot and watch while the mixture came up to a boil and then set it back to steep a little. Mama always served coffee with heavy cream.

One time one of the ladies forgot it was her turn to be co-hostess. Halfway through the meeting we spied her hustling across the field, bringing a buff roaster full of piping hot doughnuts. Another reason why we enjoyed these days was that Mama would be sure to use the good china, and we weren't allowed to wash those dishes.

Our own social life wasn't hectic. The school and church groups had socials now and then, and if you were on the refreshment committee there was much bustling about trying to decide on the menu. Many young people took piano lessons, and there were Sunday night "sings" with piano or organ. The Victrola was an important source of entertainment. We sat enraptured listening to John McCormack and Enrico Caruso, and we tried imitating Harry Lauder singing "Roamin' in the Gloamin'." There were comedy records and melodramatic songs too; I especially remember, "Hello central give me heaven, for my mama's gone up there."

We weren't allowed to frequent the movies; occasionally we went to the matinee on Saturday where Pearl White and the hero would foil the villain, or maybe the wild west show on Saturday night. Sunday's Beverly Bain and Francis X. Bushman exploits we only heard about second-hand, as Papa didn't approve of Sunday movies.

Mama didn't do a lot of fancywork, but she enjoyed making "mile-a-minute" lace, which she sewed on our camisoles and petticoats. Papa thought such fussing was silly.

"Can't see any sense in putting all that work on underwear, nobody sees it anyway." Mama would say, "It's just for prettiness," and Papa would snort, "Women!"

One day Mama fixed him. He had gone upstairs to bed early, as usual, and Mama seemed to be acting strangely, hovering near the rolling door that led to the stairway, instead of working in the kitchen or doing some patching. All of a sudden we heard a terrific roar from above, and then, "Tollie!"

Mama, a funny smug look on her face, headed for the hallway, and of course, we followed her. There, at the top of the stairs stood Papa— staid, serious Papa—in his long flannel nightshirt on which Mama had carefully sewn mile-a-minute lace around the neck, sleeves, and hem.

Above the burst of laughter I heard someone say, "You look real pretty in that nightshirt, Papa." But Mama had to rip the lace off before he'd go to bed. No fancy trimmings for him.

October

Autumn comes on like a television spectacular, but with a performance that lasts weeks instead of an hour or two. Nature's artistry surrounds us; the flamboyant colors of the oaks, maples, and sumac are breath-taking in the glow of the sun. Flowers vie with each other in their autumn garb of russet, gold, flaming red, and tawny brown. What a panorama for us to enjoy!

A poet said, "October dresses in flame and gold, Like a woman afraid of growing old." I find myself turning to bright clothes now. Of course, I'm not *really* old—74 isn't ancient—but bright colors are cheerful. I remember that my mother never would wear lavender; she said it was an old lady's color. Still, some of my favorite people wore lavender, almost as a trademark. When I was young it wasn't considered seemly to wear gaudy shades as you got older; it made you conspicuous. And when we begged to have a black dress we were told, "Time enough to wear black when you get old." My mother never wore black, either. She was so slight it would have made her look like a pencil. Blue was her favorite color. She always wore long sleeves to cover her thin arms, and the close collar at her throat was fastened with an heirloom miniature pin that she later gave me. It disturbed me to look at her blue veined hands, but now my own are veined and have age spots. Paradoxically, I'm proud of them—they show that I've worked.

Back in high school years, we made the most of fall. It was a time to hike out in the country to gather bittersweet, wild grapes, acorns, and colored leaves, and to watch the geese flying south. Caterpillars could foretell the chance of a hard winter, we thought, by the width of the dark stripe on their backs, and we tried to discover how many acorns the squirrels had stored away. The fields alongside the roads had piles of pumpkins, a promise of spicy pies and of jack-o-lanterns later on. In the country schools, children were excused to help with the potato harvest. We made a game of raking leaves and didn't consider ourselves too old to have fun jumping into the leaf piles. There were no plastic lawn bags then; the leaves were burned, and the smell spread through every neighborhood. No regulations; just be careful.

Everything was fun in those days, even helping Papa put up the storms, tacking weatherstripping around the doors, and nailing tarpaper on the back porch to make a storm shed that served as our ice box in the winter. The jugs of boiled water were kept out there whenever there was an epidemic.

Early in October, Mama usually related the details of the great Peshtigo Fire of October 8, 1871. The fire missed the cabin where she, one-year old at the time, and her parents were living. Later in life, her mother often told her of the haze that had hung over the lumberwoods country for weeks before the blaze, and of the feeling of the impending doom everyone seemed to sense. Then on a Sunday it seemed as if the heavens opened up to rain flames and smoke. Panic ensued as families ran for the river in a vain effort to save themselves. The entire village was consumed by fire and about 1,200 people lost their lives.

Mama told us how her father helped bury the unidentified dead in a mass grave and worked with others making rough boxes to bury those who were identified. The horrible sights were too much for my grandfather. He moved his family back to Jacksonport and carried on as a timber cruiser there.

We had heard that story so often we weren't impressed in our early years. We knew it had happened on the very night of the great Chicago Fire, which started, it was said, when Mrs. O'Leary's cow kicked over a lantern in her stall. Mama's stories had a dramatic flair that made you see and feel what had happened, but to us, hearing it frequently, it seemed to be just another story. It wasn't until we were grown that we realized the full import of the experience. When I visited Peshtigo with my sisters a couple of years ago, we saw evidence of that horror—saw the mass grave in the cemetery and other artifacts and mementoes at the museum in the old Congregational church. We were truly awed.

As youngsters, we always welcomed any opportunity to have a party on Friday nights, and Columbus Day was as good an excuse as any to celebrate, even if there was disagreement over whether it was Columbus or Leif Erikson who discovered America. Columbus Day was always celebrated on the 12th, when we recited, "In fourteen hundred and ninety-two, Columbus sailed the ocean blue." We tried to imagine what it would be like not really knowing if you were going to sail off the edge of the world.

The days were getting shorter, and in our neighborhood, and most of the others in town, kids were no longer allowed to play out after supper. Lamps were lit, supper dishes done, and the floor swept. Mama set the sponge for the bread she would bake next day; coal, wood, kindling, and water were carried inside. We sat around the dining room table, where the light from the nickel lamp fell on our work—arithmetic problems, history lessons, poems to "learn by heart." A bowl of snow apples was brought up from one of the barrels in the cellar and sometimes Papa would pop corn for us in the screen popper over the coals in the range. Grandma rocked and crocheted bedroom slippers for us. Papa read the paper before going up to bed early, 8:30 at latest. Mama worked through the overflowing darning basket, then read her chapter in the Bible before she went to bed. It was a wonderful time to enjoy our favorite books like *Little Women* or *Pollyanna and the Glad Game*, and to imagine what it would be like to live in a family like one of those.

Hallowe'en was coming, and we spotted our pumpkins, which Papa would carve into jack-o-'lanterns for us. We had committee meetings at school to plan Hallowe'en parties—the games we would play and the refreshments, usually doughnuts and cider. When we were old enough to go out, we dressed as witches or ghosts, and went in neighborhood groups, with the bigger kids looking out for the young ones. I'll never forget my first Hallowe'en night out, when my friends Babe and Elsie and I decided we would take up the neighborhood boys' challenge to walk through the Haunted House.

The house was set far back from the street, its gaping windows partly hidden by ruined shutters, the fan-light over the wide front door long since shattered by stones pegged by mischievous boys. The feeble glow from the street light at the corner outlined a crumbled chimney, and fallen bricks were strewn about the ground. It was a house to stir the imagination. We had always given this house a wide berth as we passed it on our way home from school, ridiculing the possibility of its being haunted. But, on this night—Hallowe'en—anything was possible.

So there we were shivering by the tumbledown steps. Then Elsie, the bravest of us, whispered hoarsely, "Come on! We'll show 'em!" and she started ahead. Her steps rang hollowly on the rickety porch. From the gate we heard the boys egging us to go on. "Yah—see, you're too scared." Elsie's hand reached for the door knob, and we trembled even more as the door creaked open. We followed close upon Elsie's heels and edged inside. The quivering sense of fear expanded; surely we had been foolish to have let ourselves be drawn into this eerie dare.

The wind whistled through broken panes and there were other ghostly sounds, tree branches tapping the walls, and squeaking floor-boards. When our eyes accustomed themselves to the gloom, we could distinguish shrouded forms of furniture in the chilly room. Then from upstairs came the sound of measured footsteps, and at the same moment a ghastly beam of light floated about the room, resting momentarily on the table top, the mantel, the Morris chair. A tall dark shadow seemed to appear at the top of the staircase.

With piercing screams we darted out the open door and flew down the walk to the gate where the boys were waiting. Facing their derision was a lot easier than enduring the weird going-on inside. "There's someone upstairs in there," we chattered. The boys pooh-poohed our story, but none of them made a move to disprove us. When I saw Charley's flashlight, I realized what had caused the bouncing beam of light inside. I was about to berate him, when the window in Mr. Hiller's house next door banged open.

His rough voice bellowed, "Hey, you kids get away from my premises. Don't you try any of your gol-durned tricks on me!" Simultaneously, we heard muffled shots, and as we ran lickety-split away from the dreaded place, I felt a stinging blow on my leg. Rock-salt! I began to sniffle, but Elsie grabbed my hand and admonished me, "Don't be a cry-baby. Let's get out of here fast. He's just a mean old man." Babe grabbed my other hand and, thus fortified, half-hopping and limping, we escaped. By the time we reached the next corner the pain was subsiding.

We darted through a yard, a short cut towards home, but I was unceremoniously brought up short by a clothesline as I ran. It caught me across the throat and I would have fallen backwards had Elsie and Babe not grabbed me. Sobbing, I let them help me on our way until we came to the horse-block for the courthouse where we could sit down to regain breath and composure. I was not sure I cared for this Hallowe'en fun.

The town clock struck the half-hour. "I've got to get home," I blubbered. The girls, evidently feeling that they too had had enough, agreed.

As we parted at Babe's corner, I thought I saw a ghostly white form moving toward their woodshed. I heard a stifled scream as Babe flew into the house and slammed the door after her.

With my heart virtually in my throat, I tried to convince myself of my bravery as I trotted the short distance to my own house. With every step I imagined strange creatures lurking in the bushes, and I heard ghoulish sounds in the creaking branches and banging woodshed doors.

I was halfway past the cherry orchard that separated our house from Hutto's when a black hooded form appeared suddenly and a hollow voice called out, "Who-oo-oo are you-oo-oo?"

All my previous frights were as nothing, as I gazed at this apparition. I tried to scream, but the sound froze in my throat and out came a tiny bleat. I squeaked "Oh, please!" and backed up to get away. Then the black hood was lowered and I saw my mother laughing and removing the old black cape that made her look like a witch. "Really scared you, didn't I?" she chuckled. "How do you like Hallowe'ening?"

I drew a deep breath of relief and reassurance. "Oh, you scared the living daylights out of me! Was that Babe's mother, too, over by their woodshed?"

Hand in hand we walked on home, with me enjoying the telling and Mama enjoying hearing how much fun I'd had on my first Hallowe'en out.

All sorts of superstitions seemed intensified at this time of year. If we could get the 25 cents together, three or four of us would go up to see Mrs. Anger, who told fortunes with cards. Besides the dire or happy predictions she made, she was great entertainment, and we loved her. We sent away for books telling us how to read palms and tea leaves, and to interpret dreams. One year we got a Ouija board. Papa didn't approve of monkeying around with such foolishness; it was simply tempting fate, he thought. We didn't really believe the superstitions we practiced, but all the same, we'd rap on wood to prevent bad luck. If we dropped a piece of bread on the floor, it meant good luck, but if it fell buttered side down, that was bad. You hurriedly made a wish before you picked it up and went to throw it to the birds. If two people reached for a slice of bread at the same time, it meant company was coming. If you took a slice when you already had one on your plate, that meant someone was coming hungry. The heel of the bread was considered especially lucky, and some folks saw to it that when there was company to dinner a member of the family got the heel, to keep the luck in the family. You were warned never to leave the knife sticking in the loaf for this would surely bring bad luck. We always felt that the man who used to hold the loaf of bread against his dirty work clothes and then cut off a chunk with his pocket knife really brought bad luck, in the form of germs. We'd heard that "horror" story many times.

We were always interested to learn how other folks' households ran. We were surprised to find that when some families fried potatoes for supper, they sliced them into the iron frying pan and chopped them with a baking powder can, or that some folks relished home-rendered lard or bacon drippings on their bread. Verna visited a family one evening whose supper consisted of a loaf of heavy dark bread and one huge bowl of soup into which each member dipped his own spoon. Some folks enjoyed having corn meal mush each night; others thrived on salt pork, and dumplings in one home might be light as a feather, while in another they preferred the solid kind. It was even fun to watch how the neighbor girls washed their dishes—whether they washed all the silver under the suds and rinsed all at one time, or lifted each knife, fork or spoon one at a time from the suds to the hot rinse water.

I remember one year when a new girl came to school around Hallowe'en time. She was so pretty, and very popular. We envied her the smart "boughten" clothes she wore, and her huge ear-puffs, made by snarling her hair and then smoothing it over. We felt a little tacky in our home-made middy blouses and pleated wool skirts. We turned up the hem of the middies and pinned them at the hips so they didn't hang loose. Our blue wool collars with white braid trim were made separate from the middies. In this way they could be removed and washed apart from the blouse, so the color didn't run. The year I inherited Vera's red flannel blouse smocked in black, I really thought I was something.

Fall is my favorite season of the year. My favorite things today aren't the same as favorites in my young days. Some favorite friends are gone; my choice in books and poetry has matured (I hope); favorite foods have to be passed up because of diets or allergies. My favorite hymn is still "Abide With Me." I recall my favorite teachers and relatives, my favorite holiday. I recall the time I nearly burned a hole in the sheet with my flashlight, trying to finish a favorite book reading under the covers. Remembering all these things we thought were fun to do and the things we planned or hoped to accomplish is sweet. But life also brings occurrences and temptations that are best forgotten. And after all, learning to forget is as important as trying to remember!

November

The raw winds and leafless trees of November bring back memories of scruffing through fallen leaves as we helped rake the yard, and then the aroma of leaf bonfires everywhere, as evening came on. The maple trees that surrounded our house were young enough so that the leaf piles weren't all that large.

Sometimes on our way home from school, as we kicked up the leaves in our path, we struck treasure — a penny someone had lost, or a big glassie marble to add to our collection. Mama didn't like our playing in the leaves because our stockings and clothes got dirty, but we felt that a little dirt never hurt anyone.

About this time of year our folks would decide that slippers weren't enough protection; we needed high shoes for cold weather — high-buttoned shoes when I was little and high-laced shoes when I reached my teens. One pair I cherished had khaki cloth tops and leather buttons. I had to do quite a bit of coaxing to get them, for they cost the tremendous price of $11 in that World War I period. They pinched my feet and caused a blister on my heel, but I didn't dare complain.

Later, in high school, the fad was heavy boots. We clumped into the assembly wearing them with heavy socks over our stockings and long underwear, with the tops of the knitted socks turned down over the boot tops. They were so warm we didn't have to wear overshoes, but our feet perspired when we sat in the schoolroom and the cold hit our toes hard once we got outside.

Mama and Papa were fussy about the quality of the clothes we wore. I can see them yet, testing a sample of material to be made into winter clothes by holding a lighted match to a corner of the goods. If the threads curled up tight, it was good wool.

At this time of year, disease often ran rampant through the town and quarantine signs appeared on many doors indicating measles, whooping cough, la grippe, typhoid fever, smallpox, chicken pox, and the dreaded diphtheria and pneumonia. Little was known about immunization; about all we were vaccinated against was smallpox and typhoid fever. One year, though, Verna contracted smallpox, so she and Mama were quarantined at home, while Papa, Vera, Marian, and I camped out in the Harbor house across the street.

Some people had the attitude that childhood diseases were inevitable, so the children might just as well "have 'em and get it over with." Grandma Samuelson used to tell of one woman who carried her baby into a home where two children lay peppered with measles. She thought this was the time to expose her child to it. The baby, however, had terrible after-effects from the disease, suffering with eye trouble for the rest of her life.

One of the biggest celebrations I ever witnessed took place in November of 1918, when the Armistice was signed. There had been a false armistice a day or two before, when bells rang, whistles blew, and everyone turned out for the big news. Then we learned that the peace hadn't yet been signed. But on the eleventh hour of the eleventh day of the eleventh month the bells and whistles sounded in earnest. What a celebration! The town went wild, and it was my first opportunity to see and take part in a snake dance in the streets.

Often the first snowstorm of the season came around Armistice Day. Fingers and toes were nipped, and chill winds sent us indoors for warmer coats and mittens. If we hadn't already donned our long fleece-lined underwear it was a must now. Our activities became house-centered. The women folk worked on pieced quilts, crazy quilts, or hooked rugs. We girls made doll clothes, and often a group of us would go to Birdie Rosenberg's house for a sewing circle. Birdie could get lovely pieces of jeweled colored velvets and satins—remnants from her folks' millinery department in the People's Store. Some of us worked on samplers or knit string washcloths. Our middy blouses and pleated skirts were like uniforms, making us equal, whether we came from lovely homes like Birdie's, or modest ones like ours.

Social life gathered a little momentum. We had hard-time parties, backward parties, old-time parties, special day parties, pot-luck and socials. Miss Knudson came to the house and fashioned winter dresses for us. I inherited Verna's red chinchilla cloth coat, when Vera outgrew it and passed it on. The folks who had kept busy knitting socks for the soldiers now turned their efforts to making scarves and tam o'shanters. We felt very grown up as we exchanged our mittens for long gauntlet gloves that we pulled over the sleeves of our coats.

Often, before the brunt of winter set in, some of Mama's relatives or old girlhood friends would come for a visit of a few days. We loved those visits, listening to stories of childhood in pioneer days, hearing them exchange recipes. Coming home from school we might find more ladies visiting, perhaps helping tie a wool comforter, or just enjoying a coffee klatch. Many times we would bring schoolgirl friends along to enjoy the goodies; sometimes we went home with friends and were provided tea parties. I remember one friend of my mother's who used to play the piano whenever she came. Her specialties were "I'll Take You Home Again, Kathleen" and "Sweet Evalina," and how she cried every time she played "My Darling Nellie Gray."

November was when we brought in the last of the garden produce, to be stored in big stone crocks for winter use. Under the cellar steps was the potato bin, with a small bin alongside reserved for cabbage, our vitamin C supply for the winter. Jars of sauerkraut and barrels of apples stood alongside the fruit jar cupboard, where displays of home-canned strawberries, raspberries, peaches, blueberries and apple sauce sparkled.

Our cellarway steps weren't the safest place to be. A door leading to the outside, which was seldom used, was at right angles to the cellar door leading from the kitchen. The shelves on both sides of the steep steps held canning equipment, steamer, and food that needed to be kept cool. And here was where Mama had what she thought were her hiding places for goodies like raisins, nuts, baking chocolate, and the like. When Mama was gone at Ladies Aid Missionary Society, W.C.T.U. or just down town, we would scrounge around those shelves for the treats we craved. If you misjudged your reach as you stretched across the stairway, you could get a nasty fall. Once a young hired girl, who was giving us a helping hand in searching for some divinity we knew Mama had hidden, fell and bruised her leg. Luckily she didn't break it, and lucky, too, that skirts were worn long enough to cover her bruise. No need advertising the fact that we'd located Mama's good hiding spots, for she'd change in a hurry. Wide-eyed and innocent, when Mama noticed Sarah limping, we volunteered the information that she had a sore bunion.

Nobody in our neighborhood had hired help very often — maybe for a month or so after a new baby came (brought, we were told, in the doctor's little black bag). Once when Mama had a spell of bad back trouble, Mrs. Fittzgibbons came for several Mondays to preside at the washboard and copper boiler. We watched with fascination as her strong hands and arms moved rhythmically up and down the ribs of the washboard, rubbing first the bar of Fels Naphtha soap on the board, then giving the most soiled spots a rubbing that no dirt could withstand. In midmorning she and Mama sat down for a spot of tea, and if we were around, we'd join them. Our tea was the cambric kind, hot water and milk with a spoonful of sugar. We loved the stories Mrs. Fittzgibbons told of things in the "ould" country. Once she even sang a merry little Irish song for us. We admired her genial appearance: red hair done in a pug at the top of her head, crisp calico skirt with a matching dressing sacque, and a voluminous gingham apron coming down to the tops of her broad black cloth-topped shoes. She wore a gray wool-fringed shawl instead of a coat, and when she went out to hang the clothes on the line, she put the shawl over her head and fastened it at the throat with one of her strong wire hairpins.

All the flour substitutes we had used to save on wheat during the Great War must have helped our nutrition, but we were happy to inhale the aroma and enjoy the flavor of all-white bread again after the Armistice. We did less complaining, even when the menu included something we didn't care for like rutabagas, which we had to learn to like.

Whenever something we didn't enjoy was served, Mama and Papa would tell us, "You don't know what you're missing." They said that, too, when we girls "spleened against" wild game in season, duck or venison. Papa enjoyed hunting. He sometimes had a duck blind and brought home two or three birds. He also went deer hunting up at Pembine, and, when he returned, we would go through his hunting jacket very thoroughly, as he always carried a bar of Baker's sweet chocolate and a bag of raisins for sustenance in case he should get lost in the woods. The only way we would eat venison was if they told us that it was steak. It smelled just like steak. If we got too "picky" Papa would say, "Someday you may be glad to have just bread and butter."

Often in the fall our high school had a carnival, and one year I was asked to take charge of the fortune telling booth. We divided the history classroom into four booths by means of screens, and three of my friends helped out. I had sent for a book on palm reading, which I studied, and so became fairly familiar with the business of heart lines and life lines and the mounts and their meaning. It wasn't too hard to fabricate the kind of a fortune our patrons wanted to hear, and as we wore masks, it didn't embarrass us.

Myrtle was a whiz at making the little table on the Ouija board zip along to the right letters; squeals and laughter came from her booth as questions were answered. Yvonne read tea leaves, while Elsie made wild predictions as she dealt out cards and interpreted their meanings — that tall dark man in your future, a sinister warning of bad luck, or a promise of a fabulous fortune. People surely got their nickel's worth when she told their fortune.

I wonder if it is just a trick of memory, or really true that winter came earlier with more snow, years ago? I remember that when I was in grade school, it was normal to expect snow drifts at Thanksgiving. We all sang lustily the familiar song:

Over the river and through the wood,
To grandmother's house we go.
The horse knows the way
To carry the sleigh,
Through the white and drifted snow.

We had no grandmother's house to go to; our only grandmother lived with us. But on that memorable Thanksgiving all the grandchildren were together, as our Aunt Grace and her four children came for the holiday. Preparations had been going on for a week.

Anticipation ran high at school, too. Our readers related the stories of the Pilgrims landing on Plymouth Rock, their suffering through the first long winter, and their gratitude for a bountiful harvest. We colored pictures in the little booklets we made to take home, and memorized the verse:

Said Old Gentleman Gay,
"On Thanksgiving Day,
If you want to be happy,
Give something away."

When our booklets were neat and the stories and poems copied in fair imitation of Miss Mae Minor's beautiful Palmer Method handwriting, she would stamp "Good Work," on it. (We saved the Good Work papers and when we had a hundred, we'd get a prize.)

At home, helping with the holiday preparations made Thanksgiving seem to come much faster. We prepared the suet, raisins, citron, apples, currants, and beef for the mincemeat using the two-bladed chopping knife and mixing everything together with cinnamon, cloves, allspice, and nutmeg in the huge wooden chopping bowl. We kept the woodbox filled for the big black range, carried pails of water from the pump outside the back door, and brought scuttles of coal from the woodshed for the base burner.

On Thanksgiving morning we were up early, but we received scant attention. We dished up our own oatmeal from the double boiler and munched on rusks made of buttered and cinnamon-sprinkled rolls, toasted in the oven. Two of the girls decided they wouldn't eat any breakfast so they'd have a better appetite for the feast. They were to rue that, though, as the long wait till the turkey was done left them faint and almost too nauseated to eat.

We watched spellbound, as the turkey was readied for the oven. Turkey was a once-a-year meat in those days. You ordered it either from Mrs. Huxford's Market or direct from a farmer, and it came still sporting its long neck and head. Occasionally we'd hear about a family that raised its turkey from small on and grew so attached to it that they had to ask a neighbor to chop off its head. Then when it was carried to the table, all brown and succulent, some of the family were so disturbed, they lost their appetites for turkey and ate potatoes and squash instead.

The task of tweezing out all of the black pinfeathers was done the night before, and the bird was stored overnight in the back shed, the coolest storage spot we had in winter. In the morning, we were relieved to find it hadn't been stolen.

"Run outside and play, children," we heard time and again, all through the morning. We didn't want to miss the activities in the house, but we'd go and play fox and geese, build a snow man, or make angels in the snow. Then, when we could rightly claim to be cold, we got back into the fascinating kitchen. Rubbers, leggin's, long black stockings, and even the hated long underwear were soaked through from the wet snow, so we had to change and hang the wet things around the coal stove to dry, meanwhile playing flinch, old maid or checkers.

The day dragged on for us, but all the while the savory smells heightened, coming in waves when the oven door was opened to baste the turkey. Some of the recipes Mama followed were printed in the *Sturgeon Bay Cook Book*, published in 1903. In addition to telling how to make all sorts of wonderful things, that old oilcloth-covered book carried many memorable ads, like the one that said, "A good pumpkin pie contains spices, and the same is true in a well-kept Jewelry Store. We have some spicy things we want you to see." Peerless Ranges were advertised, as was Wingold Flour. Falk and Buchan's ad read, "You must have good flour to get good results from the recipes. We have the flour and would like to see you. Also corn-meal, whole wheat flour, graham, breakfast foods, etc." One of Papa's cousins, a news dealer and stationer, offered high grade confectionery, cigars, wallpaper, meals, lunches, and board by the day of the week. And the Home Bakery, J. Frederickson, Prop., suggested, "A nice cake for your child's birthday party. Baked and decorated."

Soon it was time to open the big table in the dining room to its full length and put the extra leaves in. Next, the table pad was put down and then Great-Aunt Effie's linen tablecloth with the red-striped border was smoothed over. The best china came down from the cupboard, the cut-glass compotes, celery dishes, and fruit bowls. The best silver was taken from the flannel-lined cases and a lace doily was placed at the center of the table under a bowl of polished fruit. The largest linen napkins were used, and the best glassware.

Dinner time was drawing closer, and there was an almost feverish activity in the kitchen: potatoes, boiling and almost ready for mashing; sweet potatoes, candied on the back of the range; rutabagas, hubbard squash, and creamed onions; luscious golden gravy, smooth as silk; crisp cole slaw, pickled crab apples, spiced peaches, and crunch celery standing tall in the cut-glass holder; and the inevitable mold of quivery jelly, turned out on the high compote. Somehow all of this, and more, was arranged on the table. There was a variety of breads, white, spice, and corn-meal, and rolls, besides butter and milk, and finally, the treat we had all been waiting for, the bird itself, crispy brown, fragrant and juicy, with the delectable stuffing oozing out just waiting to be scooped into the serving bowl.

We took our seats and the buzz of conversation hushed. We bowed our heads while Mama said grace, then each in turn related what he or she had to be thankful for. Then began the passing of dishes. What plate-fuls of food! What enormous appetites on that day! Almost—but not quite—were we too full for pie—golden pumpkin, criss-cross raspberry, hot mince. We had to sample a bit of each. The pies had been baked the day before so the oven would be free for the turkey. Some housewives made several pies at a time and froze them out on the covered back porch for future use. We often heard the story of the woman who marked her top crusts so she'd be able to distinguish them, but couldn't remember if the "T.M." stood for " 'tis mince" or "tain't mince."

The afternoon was almost over. We children dressed warm for a romp in the snow, while Mama and Aunt Grace did the dishes. Children weren't trusted with the best china. It would be another year before we feasted on turkey again. But we had the blessings of love and home and family every day, and as we went through the kitchen we joined Mama in singing, "Praise God from whom all blessings flow." This was a Thanksgiving to remember.

December

December means business, right from the start. We wake to a winter wonderland of bare tree branches and shrubs transformed with cottony puffs of snow. The ice on the bay moves out and in again, before melding to a solid mass. Birds storm the feeders; colorful grosbeaks quarrel with the sparrows and nuthatches to see who can consume the most sunflower seeds. Ducks make frequent foraging pilgrimages along the shore in search of food, or waddle across the ice-floes, when friendly hands throw corn to them. Sea gulls are rarely seen. Occasionally a big boat comes through the channel. Just before sunrise the cardinal appears with his mate; his coloring is repeated in the glow of the eastern sky. Winter sunsets, too, are something to behold, with their promise of refreshing beauty again tomorrow.

Here in Door County we learn to adjust to weather variations. We stay close to the fire if we've no reason to go out. We prepare for the chance of being snowbound, stocking up on food and fuel in anticipation of the inevitable blizzard. Sometimes a storm can give us a free day with the chance to wrap gifts, address cards, maybe do a little early Christmas baking, or finish a gift we're making. All of December, it seems, comes under the influence of the rush and flurry of Christmas. As days grow shorter, the sounds, the sights, the smells, and the spirit of Christmas fill the air.

Christmas is a time for remembering. I think back to my early school days, when Christmas always seemed a long time in coming. Our social activities were limited to preparing programs for school and Sunday School. There were rehearsals after school and on Saturdays, and everyone had a part to learn. At school, the period following afternoon recess on the day before the Christmas vacation began was set aside for our program and party, with treats brought from home, as well as some furnished by the teacher. In the eighth grade, we had a very serious and strict teacher who decided to resign at Christmas time. As I recall, it all had to do with some conflict with the school board about her wages. To our amazement, she became a very human, warm person at that last Christmas party, laughing, and tossing apples to us as part of the game. All of a sudden, we hated to see her go.

Sometimes the theme of the school program was "Christmas in Many Lands," and then we put together our versions of what Dutch, French, German, Scandinavian and other nationalities wore. One year we had a pageant called "Why the Chimes Rang." And always we would read *The Bird's Christmas Carol*, *The Littlest Angel*, and Dickens's *Christmas Carol*.

School always ended two or three days before Christmas, to allow the teachers to get home for the holidays. We carried home our party treats and exchange gifts, to put under our own tree, and related the events of the afternoon to Mama, being sure to describe the kind of dress the teacher had worn and the gifts she had received—a pile of handkerchiefs, fancy toilet soap, penwipers, and pin cushions. Mama usually sent a box of homemade fondant.

Years later, as a country schoolma'am myself, I felt the responsibility of getting up an evening program, when all the papas and mamas would come to hear their children speak or sing. I got in "Dutch" once, when the supervising teacher walked in on me as we were rehearsing. The youngsters were sent back to their classes, and I was given my first bad report. But my school board director made a special trip into town to explain that the teachers had been given permission to shorten classes and use the free time practicing. Otherwise we would have only a half-hour noon break in which to practice because the sleigh-bus called for the children early in order to get them home before dark. No matter how much or how little we practiced, though, every program had its mishaps. Someone got scared and started crying, someone else forgot his lines, sometimes the curtains fell down, but it was all taken in good spirits. And the children thought the treat—candy canes, or bags of candy and nuts—made it all worthwhile.

In the Sunday school pageants we took the parts of shepherds, angels, and wise men. Some of us also had "pieces" to speak and usually there were several acrostic songs, with each child holding up his or her letter card while speaking or singing. "Away in a Manger" was the song the little folks were given, and "Silent Night" and "Oh Come All Ye Faithful" were musts. We rehearsed the program for several weeks. The Sunday school teachers sometimes had difficulty keeping discipline in the hubbub. But by Christmas Eve most of the problems had been ironed out, and we arrived at church in our home-made costumes with our "best" dresses or suits worn underneath. The bulges from our wrapped-over long underwear legs may have detracted from the appearance of the angels, and sometimes our tinseled wings and haloes slipped a bit; but the story of that first Christmas rang out clear and true.

Of course, for many weeks, our minds had been full of thoughts about the gifts we would give and receive. We made frequent excuses to stop at the library after school and on Saturdays, so that we could come the long way home and gaze into the store windows, wishing and speculating on whether the longed-for doll, skates, or other special gift, missing from the window display, had possibly been put away for one of us. The "wishing books," that came from the stores some called Sears and Sawbuck and Monkey Ward, were almost worn out with looking. Supper table conversation buzzed with hints of secrets, plans, and reports of what our friends expected under their trees. We fussed less about chores, growing more and more cooperative as the 25th drew near.

Many evenings we went off by ourselves to finish up the gifts we made for each other: pen-wipers; needle-books; pincushions; handkerchiefs with embroidered initials; camisoles with baby ribbon run through the beading and with beauty pins for fastening; organdy dickies trimmed with lazy-daisy flowers; yards of spool knitting made into table mats. A few evenings before Christmas, we made candy to box for teacher gifts or for special friends.

Long hours of preparation went into the home-made gifts. One year there was a doll house, made duplex style so two little girls could play with it at the same time. We always enjoyed getting doll furniture and curtains for the little windows. Raggedy Ann and Andy dolls were among our favorites. ("I love you" was embroidered on Raggedy Ann's heart.) Our Flexible Flyer sleds and clamp-on skates were refurbished to be used through more winters as the younger children grew ready for them. We stressed the fact that it was the thought that counted, and we didn't dwell on what we couldn't have, because very few others could have those things either.

Not all of our gifts were homemade, however, for Papa usually gave each of us Christmas spending money. Fifty cents was the enormous sum, as I remember, and how rich we felt as we made our way downtown. How exciting the stores were, with their red and green garlands and tempting window displays of things we all hoped to see under our tree come Christmas morning. We all started out together, but separated when we got to the stores as everything had to be very secret. There was a temptation to splurge at the candy counter, for we could easily persuade ourselves that Papa would appreciate a gift of his favorite rock candy, or horehound. But we knew he'd be bringing home paper sacks of candy, including the chocolate drops we adored, as well as walnuts, Brazil nuts, and peanuts. So I would buy materials for a doll bunting, and ribbon with which to trim it, for Marian's doll. New hair ribbons for the girls, a "cameo" brooch for Mama, a stick pin for Papa's tie, and a thimble for Grandma, and, if I'd hoarded any of my own pennies, it all came out even.

Mama always had tissue paper for wrapping, and we used red or green yarn to tie our packages. Sometimes we made pom-poms or tiny yarn dolls at the end of the ties. Often we wrote special verses to go with each gift.

Saturday morning, about two weeks before Christmas, every young person in the neighborhood "slicked up" and bundled up, ready for a big day—the arrival of Santa. Singly or in groups, we all plodded down to the depot to wait for the Ahnapee and Western train that would bring him in. A horde of excited girls and boys would welcome him and later stand in line at Rosenberg's department store to tell him what they wanted for Christmas.

When we heard the long, deep whistle, we knew that the train was crossing the railroad bridge. We shivered with excitement and the cold as we stretched on tiptoe straining to catch the first glimpse of the huge iron horse that belched black smoke as it roared into the depot.

"Ho! Ho! Ho!" There he was, sure enough, Santa with white whiskers and a bright red suit. We crowded closer, and those of us who were not too shy stepped up to greet him and to receive the bags of candy and nuts his sack held for "all good little boys and girls." Then as he led the parade like the Pied Piper of Hamelin, we fell in line and marched up Cedar Street to Rosenberg's, lustily singing "Jingle Bells."

A new dress for Christmas was a must. I always longed for a blue velvet, but with two older sisters who were likely to have outgrown their last year's dresses, most often one of them would be refurbished for me. But with new hair ribbons, a ribboned sash, and perhaps new shoes, I was satisfied with my "new" outfit. Besides, your dress was usually covered with the angel, shepherd, or wise man's costume for the program at church. Usually a week or so after Thanksgiving our favorite dressmaker, Anna Knudson, could spare us a few days to make our Christmas dresses. Anna was a wizard at sewing up a storm. We looked forward to the sewing days with their special treats like being allowed to pull out the bastings. But we didn't like the fittings, turning this way and that, and being told to stand still.

Next by way of preparations came the housecleaning; we weren't as enthusiastic about that. The carpets couldn't be taken out to be beaten on the line, because of the snow on the ground, but we swept them with salt, and sometimes sprinkled snow on them to bring out the brightness. Pictures and frames had to be cleaned with ammonia solution, and windows washed sparkling with Bon Ami. We tied cloths around the broom to gather up any stray cobwebs on walls or ceilings, and while doing so were reminded of the story of the little spiders who went creepy-creep all over the Christmas tree, leaving webs that the good fairy turned into tinsel. The "oatmeal" wallpaper — dark red, dark green, or tan — looked fresh and clean after its massage with wall-paper cleaner. The nickel trim and isinglass windows of the base burner were polished to a shine. While we were at school, Mama took down the lace curtains, washed them, and put them on the stretchers. By the time we got home they hung, starched stiff in pristine splendor, the scalloped edges where the pins had held them firmly in place attesting to the highest standard of housekeeping. Even the front door was scrubbed, so we could hang the evergreen wreath we so laboriously twined around the heavy wire frame.

Most important of all, getting ready for Christmas meant the preparation of special food. Even before Thanksgiving, the mincemeat had been readied, giving the house an anticipatory fragrance. Shortly thereafter, we were allowed to help chop citron, raisins, nuts, and figs for the fruit cakes that would be baked slowly, then wrapped and stored to mellow till Christmas. It seemed we made an endless variety of cookies, but the most fun were the gingerbread men, rolling ever so carefully the molasses, or sugar cooky dough, thriftily turning the tin cutters to cut the dough to best advantage, sprinkling the colored sugar on top. We punched holes in the tops of some, so we could run a thread through and hang them on the tree.

Nationality had a lot to do with families' food choices at Christmas. In our house, at one time or another, we had rosettes, doughnuts, kolaches, coffee cakes, kuchen, lefse, fattigman, krumkake, fruit soup, Swedish meat balls, Jule kage, Scotch raisin bread, scones, Cornish saffron bread, stollen, and many others — a conglomeration of recipes from friends, neighbors, or ancestors.

I remember how Great-Grandma gloried in preparing the holiday dinners, in training young fingers to mix, pat, or roll things her way, guiding their hands as they shaped the special neighbor gifts that were wrapped in blue tissue, with silver stars dotted all over and sent off on Christmas Eve. What a marvelous hand she was at making melt-in-your mouth divinity, chocolate fudge, or penuche. And as she worked, she supervised the making of popcorn balls or taffy pulling, or taught us how to drop sugar mints and coat them with melted chocolate. Her ingenuity was something to marvel at. She would spread boiled frosting, tinted pink, over crackers, sprinkle with nuts, and bake until light and puffy—a real treat.

One of Mama's favorites for the holiday season was chocolate-potato cake, because it kept so well, but I don't know why she was concerned about the keeping quality, since no cake lasted long with our healthy appetites. Mama always made a boiled frosting, and we watched as she dripped the hot syrup from the spoon to see if it spun a thread, before pouring it slowly on the beaten whites. Once Verna and I tried giving the egg whites an extra good whipping and ended up with their going watery and having to be thrown out. "Help" like that wasn't appreciated at all. Mama always said that if you poured melted chocolate into the frosting it thinned it down too much, so she usually covered the cake with a white frosting, then dribbled chocolate on top of it, adding a spoon of butter to the chocolate so it spread more evenly. We all loved that double frosting, especially on the chocolate-potato cake. Friends of ours had boys who had a way of assuring thick frosting on their cakes. When their mother baked, they watched for a time when she was out of the kitchen, then opened the oven door and let it slam, causing the cake to fall. Their mother couldn't understand why her cakes were a failure, when other things baked so beautifully in her range. But she made up for the fallen cake by spreading the frosting extra thick—just what the boys had been aiming for.

Finally, the day for which all this preparation took place was upon us. Although at times we thought Christmas would never come, here it was— Christmas Eve. Last minute cleaning, polishing, and baking done—the house was in readiness—with the lighted candle in the window to light the Christ Child on his way. Our family tradition called for a meatless meal on the night before Christmas, usually salmon loaf, baked potatoes, cocoa, and cookies.

Then it was hurry, hurry to get dishes done and get ready for the program at church. Walking through drifts of snow was a starry, Christmas-card pilgrimage. The church chimes rang out "Joy to the World." Christmas

185

had begun! Back home we hung up our red cambric stockings on the back of a chair, because we didn't have a mantel. We would rush into the normally cold parlor with our presents for the family and sneak longing looks at the gifts already there, under the tree that stood waiting to be decorated. One year I discovered that the letter C in Santa Claus on a box bearing my name had been made with loops at the top and bottom, just like Mama made her capital C's!

Trimming the tree was the high point of Christmas Eve, when we were big enough to be allowed to help. We were lucky to have an uncle who brought us a tree each year. Papa fastened it securely in the wooden tree stand, and carried it into the parlor. The rolling doors were left open all morning, so the heat could reach that room. Reverently we unwrapped each cherished ornament — the birds with the spun-glass tails, the colorful glass balls, the bright cardboard figures, and, eventually, the strings of lights. The sights, the colors and sounds of Christmas were all around us. We breathed in the fragrant odors as we lifted the tinsel from the box, or hung paper chains or popcorn strings from limb to limb of the tree. We added the thread spools that we had transformed into drums, the salt and flour dough figures, and the walnut shells we had glued together and wrapped in foil saved from candy boxes. Once Vera told us about the marvelous new "icicles" that Jenny Wright was going to have on her tree. (Jenny was engaged to Holman White who was manager of the new Woolworth store.) I was sent down, post haste, to buy a box of the novelties. And what a wonderful tree we had that year! Even the star on top seemed to shine brighter.

Pretty soon it was time for us to run upstairs to our cold bedroom, to climb into the bed piled high with quilts and a hot water bottle or wrapped hot flat irons at our feet, and to dream of the treats that the morning would bring. And when Christmas morning came, and we could persuade Papa and Mama it was light enough to get up, we would wait impatiently while Papa shook the grates in the coal stove and the range, and the heat began to penetrate the room. Then, wrapped in our bathrobes, we padded down the stairs to savor the beauty of the Christmas tree. Before electricity came to our house, our tree was lit with candles, which Papa would light and then stand guard with a pail of water and a dipper, in case of fire. How wonderful were those tree lights; it was as if by a miracle that those tiny strings of foil became shining icicles! Our hearts were filled with joy and love and peace. We knew we had received the blessing of Christmas.